EVERYTHING YOU NEED TO KNOW FOR PERFECT BARBECUING

This book not only makes outdoor cooking more delicious, it also makes it much easier. There are dozens of handy hints and helpful tips, including:

- How to pick what kind of grill is best for you
- How to start coals quickly and easily
- How to roast foods on a spit
- How to arrange coals for proper temperature dispersion
- How to grill foods that need frequent turning
- How to know when your food is done just the way you want it

BETTER HOMES AND GARDENS® ALL-TIME FAVORITE BARBECUE RECIPES

BETTER HOMES AND GARDENS®
ALL-TIME FAVORITE
BARBECUE RECIPES

BETTER HOMES AND GARDENS®
ALL-TIME FAVORITE BARBECUE RECIPES
*A Bantam Book / published by arrangement with
Meredith Corporation*

PRINTING HISTORY
*Better Homes and Gardens edition published February 1977
9 printings through February 1980
Better Homes and Gardens Family Book Service edition
March 1977
Bantam edition / July 1980*

Book designed by Cathy Marinaccio

*Bantam Books are published by Bantam Books, Inc. Its trade-
mark, consisting of the words "Bantam Books" and the por-
trayal of a bantam, is Registered in U.S. Patent and Trademark
Office and in other countries. Marca Registrada. Bantam
Books, Inc., 666 Fifth Avenue, New York, New York 10103.*

PRINTED IN THE UNITED STATES OF AMERICA

0 9 8 7 6 5 4 3 2 1

CONTENTS

BARBECUING
FOR EVERYONE

Getting superb results each time you barbecue—and enjoying your success—is what this book is all about. We've gathered recipes representing the best of barbecuing over the years. Enjoy sizzling steaks, ribs, grilled vegetables and breads, and savory desserts. Then help yourself to a special chapter on using small barbecue equipment, understanding various types of grills, and building and controlling coals. So whether you're an experienced barbecue enthusiast or a "sometimes backyard chef," you'll find *All-Time Favorite Barbecue Recipes* takes the guesswork out of barbecuing.

GRILLING OVER THE COALS

Type of food	Cut or portion (placed 4 inches above coals)	Weight or thickness	Temperature of coals*
Beef	Burgers	½ inch	Medium-hot Medium
		¾ inch	Medium-hot Medium
	Porterhouse, T-bone, or sirloin steak	1 inch	Medium-hot
		1½ inches	Medium-hot Medium
	Chuck blade steak	1 inch	Medium
		2½ inches	Medium
Lamb	Rib chops	1 inch	Medium
		1½ inches	Medium
	Shoulder chops	1 inch	Medium
		1½ inches	Medium
Pork	Loin chops	1 inch	Medium
		1½ inches	Medium
	Blade steak	¾ inch	Medium
	Loin back ribs or spare ribs	5–6 pounds	Medium
Ham	Fully cooked slice	½ inch	Medium-hot
		1 inch	Medium
	Canned	5 pounds	Medium
Chicken	Broiler-fryer halves	2½–3 pounds	Medium-hot
	Roasting chicken, unstuffed	3–4 pounds	Medium
Turkey	Unstuffed	6–8 pounds	Medium
		12–16 pounds	Medium
Fish	Salmon or halibut steaks	¾ inch	Medium
		1–1½ inches	Medium-hot
	Trout, snapper, or whitefish fillets	6–8 ounces each	Medium-hot Medium
Seafood	Shrimp (large)	2 pounds	Hot

*Estimate by holding hand, palm down, about 4 inches above hot coals. Count seconds you can hold position. Figure 2 seconds as Hot coals; 3 seconds for Medium-hot coals, 4 seconds for Medium coals, and 5 or 6 seconds for Slow coals.

A handy guide for barbecuing your favorite foods

Approximate total cooking times				Comments
Open grill		Covered grill		
Rare	Medium	Rare	Medium	
8–10 min.	10–12 min.	7–9 min.	8–10 min.	Four burgers per pound
10–12 min.	12–15 min.	8–10 min.	10–12 min.	
10–12 min.	12–15 min.	8–10 min.	10–12 min.	Three burgers per pound
12–15 min.	14–18 min.	10–12 min.	12–15 min.	
12–18 min.	15–20 min.	8–10 min.	10–15 min.	Check doneness by cutting a slit in meat near bone
18–20 min.	20–25 min.	10–15 min.	15–18 min.	
20–25 min.	25–30 min.	15–18 min.	18–22 min.	
12–18 min.	15–20 min.	8–10 min.	12–18 min.	
50–60 min.	55–65 min.	45–55 min.	50–60 min.	Use foil tent on open grill
	20–25 min.		20–25 min.	Check doneness by cutting a slit in meat near bone
25–30 min.	28–32 min.	20–25 min.	23–28 min.	
	22–28 min.		18–22 min.	
28–32 min.	30–35 min.	20–25 min.	25–30 min.	
	Well-done		Well-done	
	22–25 min.		18–22 min.	A wire grill basket aids in turning
	30–35 min.		25–30 min.	
	15–20 min.		15–20 min.	
			1¼–1½ hrs.	
	10–15 min.		10–15 min.	Slash fat edge of ham slice
	25–35 min.		20–30 min.	
	1½–1¾ hrs.		1¼–1¾ hrs.	Use foil tent on open grill
	45–50 min.		40–45 min.	
			2–2½ hrs.	
			3–3¾ hrs.	Meat thermometer inserted in thigh should register 185°
			3½–4½ hrs.	
	17–22 min.		15–20 min.	Use a wire grill basket
	10–17 min.		10–15 min.	
	10–17 min.		10–15 min.	Use a wire grill basket
	17–20 min.		15–17 min.	
	15–18 min.		15–18 min.	

ROTISSERIE SPECIALTIES

Type of food	Cut	Weight	Temperature of coals*
Beef	Rolled rib roast	5–6 pounds	Medium
	Tenderloin roast	2½ pounds	Medium-hot
	Eye of round	3–4 pounds	Medium-hot
	Boneless rump roast	3–4 pounds	Slow
Lamb	Leg	5–7 pounds	Medium
Pork	Boneless loin roast	5–6 pounds	Medium
	Loin back ribs or spareribs	3–4 pounds	Slow
Ham	Boneless piece	9–10 pounds	Medium
	Canned	5 pounds	Medium
Chicken	Whole	2½–3 pounds	Medium-hot Medium
Cornish Hens	4 birds	1–1½ pounds each	Medium-hot
Duckling	Whole domestic	4–6 pounds	Medium-hot
Turkey	Unstuffed	6–8 pounds	Medium
	2 rolled turkey roasts	28 ounces each	Medium-hot
	Boneless turkey roast	5–6 pounds	Medium-hot

SMOKER COOKING

Type of food	Cut or portion	Size or weight
Pork	Boneless loin roast	4–5 pounds
	6–8 loin chops	1½ inches thick (1 pound each)
	Loin back ribs or spareribs	4–5 pounds
Turkey	Ready-to-cook frozen bird, completely thawed	12–15 pounds
Fish	Salmon (fillets or red snapper)	3–4 pounds

*Estimate by holding hand, palm down, about 4 inches above hot coals. Count seconds you can hold position. Figure 2 seconds as Hot coals; 3 seconds for Medium-hot coals; 4 seconds for Medium coals, and 5 or 6 seconds for Slow coals.

Guidelines for cooking meats and poultry on a spit

Approximate roasting time			Comments
Covered grill			
Rare	Medium	Well-done	
2–2½ hrs. 40–45 min. 1¼–1½ hrs.	2½–3 hrs. 45–50 min. 1½–2 hrs. 1¼–1¾ hrs.	1½–2 hours	Have meat rolled and tied
1 hr.	1½–2 hrs.	1¾–2¼ hours	Have shank cut off short Balance diagonally on spit
		4–4½ hours 1–1¼ hours	Have meat rolled and tied Thread on spit accordion fashion
		2–2¼ hours 1¼–1½ hours	Tie securely after mounting on spit
		1½–1¾ hours 1½–2 hours	
		1½–1¾ hours	
		1½–1¾ hours	Deep foil drip pan is essential
		3¼–4½ hours 1¾–2¼ hours 2½–3½ hours	Push holding forks deep in bird Purchase frozen; thaw completely

Approximate timings when using a portable smoker**

Approximate smoking time	Doneness	Comments
4–5 hours 2–2½ hours	well-done well-done	170° on roast meat thermometer Cut slit in chop near bone to check doneness of meat
4–5 hours	well-done	
8–9 hours	185° (internal temperature	Check internal temperature at thigh with meat thermometer
2–3 hours	fully cooked	Fish will flake easily with a fork

**Check manufacturer's directions for placement of charcoal, hickory chips, and water pan.

MAIN DISHES FOR
OUTDOOR BARBECUES

If you've ever been tantalized by the smell of steaks, burgers, frankfurters, or other meats wafting through the air, you'll find much to be glad about in this section. In addition to scrumptious recipes for over-the-coals favorites, you'll discover new taste delights, too—beef short ribs, pork loin roasts, Cornish hens, salmon steaks, and many more. Try out your barbecuing skills at grilling, spit-roasting, skewer, or smoke cooking.

Beef

STEAK AND BACON TOURNEDOS

1 1- to 1½-pound beef flank
   steak
Instant unseasoned meat
   tenderizer
10 slices bacon
1 teaspoon garlic salt
½ teaspoon freshly ground
   pepper
2 tablespoons snipped parsley
1 1¾-ounce envelope hollandaise
   sauce mix
¼ teaspoon dried tarragon,
   crushed

Pound flank steak evenly about ½ inch thick. Apply meat tenderizer according to package directions. Meanwhile, cook bacon till almost done, but not crisp.

Sprinkle flank steak with garlic salt and pepper. Score steak diagonally, making diamond-shaped cuts. Place bacon strips lengthwise on flank steak. Sprinkle

7

with parsley. Roll up as for jelly roll, starting at narrow end. Skewer with wooden picks at 1-inch intervals. Cut into eight 1-inch slices with serrated knife.

Grill over *medium* coals for 8 minutes. Turn; grill 7 minutes more for rare. Meanwhile, in saucepan prepare hollandaise sauce mix according to package directions, adding tarragon to dry mix. Remove picks from meat slices. Serve hollandaise sauce with meat. Makes 4 servings.

VEGETABLE-BEEF ROLLS

1 beaten egg
1½ pounds ground beef
½ cup shredded carrot
¼ cup finely chopped onion
¼ cup finely chopped green
   pepper
¼ cup finely chopped celery
½ teaspoon salt
   Dash pepper
12 slices bacon
½ cup Italian salad dressing

Combine egg and ground beef; mix well. Divide meat mixture into six portions. On waxed paper flatten each meat portion into a 6x4-inch rectangle. Combine carrot, onion, green pepper, celery, salt, and pepper. Divide vegetable mixture into six portions. Pat one vegetable portion onto each meat rectangle. Roll up each rectangle as for jelly roll. Wrap two slices of bacon around each of the rolls and secure with wooden picks.

Place rolls in shallow baking dish. Pour salad dressing over; let stand at room temperature about 1 hour, turning occasionally to moisten all sides. Remove meat rolls from dressing, reserving marinade. Grill rolls over *medium* coals for 20 to 25 minutes, turning to grill all sides and brushing with reserved dressing occasionally. Remove picks before serving. Makes 6 servings.

LEMON PEPPER FLANK PINWHEELS

2 1-pound beef flank steaks
½ cup Burgundy
¼ cup cooking oil
¼ cup soy sauce
1 tablespoon lemon pepper
1 tablespoon Worcestershire
   sauce
Few drops bottled hot pepper
   sauce
8 cherry tomatoes *or* mushroom
   caps

Pound each flank steak to a 10x8-inch rectangle. Cut each rectangle into four 10x2-inch strips.

In bowl combine Burgundy, cooking oil, soy sauce, lemon pepper, Worcestershire, and pepper sauce. Place meat strips in plastic bag; set in a deep bowl. Pour wine mixture over meat; close bag. Marinate 4 to 6 hours or overnight in refrigerator, turning twice.

Drain meat; reserve marinade. Loosely roll each strip around a cherry tomato or mushroom cap, starting with short side. Skewer securely with wooden picks.

Grill pinwheels over *medium* coals for 15 minutes. Turn meat; grill about 10 minutes more for rare. Baste with marinade often. Remove picks. Makes 8 servings.

SMOKED FRENCH PEPPER STEAK

Hickory chips
2 tablespoons cracked
    pepper
1 2-pound beef sirloin steak,
    cut 1½ inches thick
¼ cup butter *or* margarine
2 tablespoons lemon juice
1 teaspoon Worcestershire
    sauce
½ teaspoon garlic powder
¼ teaspoon salt

About an hour before cooking time, soak hickory chips in enough water to cover. Drain.

Press cracked pepper into both sides of steak, using the heel of your hand or the flat side of a cleaver.

In saucepan over coals melt butter; stir in lemon juice, Worcestershire, garlic powder, and salt. Remove from coals.

Add damp hickory chips to *medium-hot* coals; place steak on grill and lower smoke hood. Grill steak for 17 to 20 minutes, brushing occasionally with lemon sauce. Turn meat; grill, covered, 15 to 17 minutes more for rare to medium-rare. Heat reserved lemon sauce. Slice steak; spoon sauce over slices. Makes 6 servings.

PEPPY CHUCK STEAK GRILL

1 2- to 3-pound beef chuck steak,
    cut 1 inch thick
½ cup cooking oil
½ cup dry red wine
2 tablespoons catsup
2 tablespoons molasses
2 tablespoons finely snipped
    candied ginger
1 clove garlic, minced
1 teaspoon salt
¼ teaspoon pepper

Slash fat edges of steak, being careful not to cut into meat. Place in shallow baking dish. Combine cooking oil, wine, catsup, molasses, ginger, garlic, salt, and pepper. Pour over steak. Cover; let stand 3 hours at room temperature of 6 hours, in refrigerator, turning several times.

Drain steak, reserving marinade. Pat excess moisture from steak with paper toweling.

Grill steak over *medium* coals for about 20 minutes on each side for rare; about 25 minutes on each side for medium-rare. Brush occasionally with reserved marinade.

Remove meat to serving platter. Carve across grain in thin slices. Makes 4 to 6 servings.

LEMON-MARINATED CHUCK ROAST

1 4-pound beef chuck pot roast,
    cut 1½ inches thick
1 teaspoon grated lemon
    peel
½ cup lemon juice
⅛ cup cooking oil
2 tablespoons sliced green
    onion with tops
4 teaspoons sugar
1½ teaspoons salt
1 teaspoon Worcestershire
    sauce
1 teaspoon prepared mustard
⅛ teaspoon pepper

Score fat edges of roast. Place meat in shallow baking dish. Combine lemon peel and juice, cooking oil, green onion, sugar, salt, Worcestershire, mustard, and pepper. Pour over roast. Cover; let stand 3 hours at room temperature or overnight in the refrigerator, turning roast several times.

Remove roast from marinade, reserving marinade. Pat excess moisture from roast with paper toweling.

Grill roast over *medium-hot* coals 17 to 20 minutes. Turn; cook 17 to 20 minutes more for rare to medium-rare. Heat reserved marinade on grill.

Remove roast to serving platter. Carve across the grain into thin slices. Spoon marinade over. Serves 6 to 8.

ONION-STUFFED STEAK

2 1¼- to 1½-pound porterhouse
    steaks, cut 1½ inches thick
    or 1 2-pound sirloin steak,
    cut 1½ inches thick
½ cup chopped onion
1 large clove garlic, minced
1 tablespoon butter
    or margarine
  Dash celery salt
  Dash pepper
¼ cup dry red wine
2 tablespoons soy sauce
1 cup sliced fresh mushrooms
2 tablespoons butter
    or margarine

Slash fat edges of steak at 1-inch intervals, being care-ful not to cut into meat. Slice pockets in each side of meat, cutting almost to bone.

In skillet cook onion and garlic in the 1 tablespoon butter. Add celery salt and pepper. Stuff pockets with onion mixture; skewer closed. Mix wine and soy sauce; brush on steak. Grill over *medium-hot* coals for 15 minutes; brush often with soy mixture. Turn; grill 10 to 15 minutes more for rare. Brush often with soy mixture. In small skillet cook mushrooms in the 2 tablespoons butter till tender. Slice steak across grain; pass the mushrooms and spoon atop steak. Makes 4 servings.

RICE-STUFFED FLANK STEAK

1 1- to 1¼-pound beef flank
    steak
½ teaspoon unseasoned meat
    tenderizer
¼ cup chopped onion
¼ cup chopped celery
2 tablespoons butter *or*
    margarine
½ cup water
1 tablespoon curry powder
1 teaspoon instant beef
    bouillon granules
¼ cup quick-cooking rice

Score meat diagonally on both sides; pound to an 11x9-inch rectangle. Sprinkle with tenderizer, salt, and pepper.

In saucepan cook onion and celery in butter till tender. Add water, curry, and bouillon; stir in rice. Bring to boiling; cover. Remove from heat; let stand 5 minutes.

Spread mixture on meat; roll up as for jelly roll, starting at short side. Tie with string both lengthwise and crosswise.

Insert spit rod lengthwise through center of steak. Adjust holding forks; test balance. Place *medium* coals on both sides of drip pan. Attach spit; position drip pan under meat. Turn on motor: lower hood or cover with foil tent. Roast over *medium* coals till done, about 50 minutes. Remove strings. Makes 4 servings.

SPIT-ROASTED CHATEAUBRIAND

1 2- to 2½-pound beef
    tenderloin
1 cup crumbled blue cheese
    (4 ounces)
1 tablespoon brandy

Trim fat from surface of roast. Make a slanting cut,
2 inches deep, the full length of the roast with a sharp,
narrow-bladed knife held at a 45-degree angle. Make
another cut, just as before, along opposite side.

Blend blue cheese and brandy together. Spread
cheese mixture in the two slashed openings. Securely
tie string around the roast at both ends and the middle.

Insert spit rod lengthwise through center of roast.
Adjust holding forks; test balance. Insert meat thermometer near center of roast, not touching metal rod.
Place *hot* coals on both sides of drip pan. Attach spit;
position drip pan under meat. Turn on motor; lower
hood or cover with foil tent. Grill over *hot* coals till
thermometer registers 130° for rare (about 45 minutes), 150° for medium-rare (about 50 minutes), and
160° for medium-medium well (55 to 60 minutes).
Remove string. Makes 6 to 8 servings.

MARINATED HICKORY-SMOKED CHUCK ROAST

1 2-pound beef chuck pot roast,
    cut 1¼ inches thick
5 cloves garlic, peeled
¼ cup cooking oil
¼ cup wine vinegar
1 tablespoon Worcestershire
    sauce
½ teaspoon salt
½ teaspoon dried basil, crushed
¼ teaspoon pepper
    Several dashes bottled
        hot pepper sauce
    Hickory chips

Stud roast with garlic by inserting tip of knife in meat and pushing cloves into meat as you remove knife. Make sure garlic cloves are evenly spaced.

In bowl mix oil, vinegar, Worcestershire, salt, basil, pepper, and hot pepper sauce. Place meat in plastic bag; set in shallow baking dish. Pour marinade over meat; close bag. Marinate 6 to 8 hours or overnight in refrigerator; turning roast occasionally.

About an hour before cooking soak hickory chips in enough water to cover; drain chips. Drain meat, reserving marinade. Pat excess moisture from meat with paper toweling. Arrange *medium-slow* coals around drip pan. Add hickory chips to coals. Place roast over drip pan on grill. Lower hood. Grill 25 minutes. Brush occasionally with marinade and add additional hickory chips. Turn roast; grill 20 minutes more for medium, brushing with marinade. Season to taste; remove garlic. Serves 6.

RIB ROAST BARBECUE

1   5- to 6-pound boned and rolled
    beef rib roast
½   cup Burgundy
½   cup vinegar
¼   cup cooking oil
¼   cup finely chopped onion
2   tablespoons sugar
1   tablespoon Worcestershire
    sauce
1½ teaspoons salt
½   teaspoon dry mustard
¼   teaspoon pepper
¼   teaspoon chili powder
¼   teaspoon dried thyme, crushed
1   clove garlic, minced
    Several drops bottled hot
    pepper sauce

Place meat in plastic bag; set in deep bowl. Combine remaining ingredients. Pour over meat; close bag. Marinate 6 to 8 hours or overnight in refrigerator; turn several times.

Drain meat; reserve marinade. Pat excess moisture from meat with paper toweling. Insert spit rod through center of roast. Adjust holding forks; test balance. Insert meat thermometer near center of roast but not touching metal rod. Place *medium* coals around drip pan. Attach spit; position drip pan under meat. Turn on motor; lower hood or cover with foil tent. Roast over *medium* coals till meat thermometer registers 140° for rare (2 to 2½ hours), 160° for medium, and 170° for well-done. Brush frequently with marinade during the last 30 minutes of roasting. Let stand 15 minutes before slicing. If desired, heat remaining marinade and pass with meat. Makes 15 to 20 servings.

HOT-STYLE EYE OF ROUND

1 3-pound beef eye of round
    roast
  Instant unseasoned meat
    tenderizer
1 cup hot-style catsup
½ cup water
2 tablespoons Worcestershire
    sauce
1 clove garlic, minced
½ teaspoon chili powder
¼ teaspoon salt

Sprinkle all sides of roast evenly with tenderizer, using ½ teaspoon per pound of meat. To ensure penetration, pierce all sides deeply at ½-inch intervals with long-tined fork. In saucepan combine catsup, water, Worcestershire, garlic, chili powder, and salt. Simmer 5 minutes.

Insert spit rod through center of roast. Adjust holding forks; test balance. Insert meat thermometer near center of roast, not touching metal rod. Place *medium-hot* coals around drip pan. Attach spit; position drip pan under meat. Turn on motor; lower hood or cover with foil tent. Roast over *medium-hot* coals till thermometer registers 140° for rare, about 1½ hours. Brush with sauce during last 30 minutes. Heat sauce; pass with meat. Serves 8.

CORNED BEEF BARBECUE DINNER

1 3-pound piece corned beef for
   oven roasting
6 medium baking potatoes
1 envelope dry onion soup mix
½ cup butter *or* margarine,
   softened
½ cup sugar
¼ cup vinegar
3 tablespoons prepared mustard
   Dash salt
1 cup dairy sour cream
¼ cup milk
2 tablespoons prepared mustard

Unwrap and rinse corned beef. Arrange *medium* coals around edge of grill. Place beef on heavy-duty foil drip pan on grill. Close hood; grill for 1½ hours. Scrub potatoes but do not peel. Cut each in 3 or 4 lengthwise slices. Set aside 3 tablespoons soup mix. Blend together remaining soup mix and butter. Spread mixture over potato slices. Reassemble potatoes. Wrap each in a square of the heavy-duty foil. Place at edges of grill. Grill, hood down, along with meat for 45 to 60 minutes more; turn potatoes once.

Meanwhile, in saucepan mix sugar, vinegar, 3 tablespoons mustard, and salt. Bring to boiling; stir till sugar dissolves. Brush over meat during last few minutes of grilling. Just before serving, mix sour cream, milk, reserved soup mix, and 2 tablespoons mustard. Heat through, stirring occasionally. *Do not boil.*

Unwrap potatoes. Arrange meat and potatoes on serving platter. Serve with sour cream sauce. Makes 6 servings.

BRAZILIAN BARBECUED BEEF

1 4-pound beef chuck pot roast,
    cut 2 to 2½ inches thick
1 cup catsup
⅓ cup vinegar
¼ cup cooking oil
2 tablespoons instant coffee
    crystals
1 teaspoon salt
1 teaspoon chili powder
1 teaspoon celery seed
½ teaspoon pepper
⅛ teaspoon garlic powder
3 or 4 dashes bottled hot
    pepper sauce

Slash fat edges of meat, being careful not to cut into meat. Place roast in shallow baking dish. In small bowl combine catsup, vinegar, oil, coffee crystals, salt, chili powder, celery seed, pepper, garlic powder, hot pepper sauce, and ½ cup water; pour over roast. Cover; refrigerate 6 to 8 hours or overnight, turning roast several times. Remove roast from marinade, reserving marinade. Remove excess moisture from roast with paper toweling. Grill roast over *medium* coals for 20 to 25 minutes. Turn roast; grill 10 minutes. Brush roast with marinade. Grill for 10 to 15 minutes more for rare to medium rare, brushing occasionally with marinade. Heat remaining marinade.

To serve, carve meat across the grain in thin slices. Pass heated marinade. Makes 6 to 8 servings.

WINED-AND-DINED BEEF ROAST

1 clove garlic, minced
3 tablespoons cooking oil
½ cup dry red wine
2 tablespoons lemon juice
1 teaspoon dried basil, crushed
½ teaspoon dry mustard
1 3-pound beef chuck pot roast,
    cut 1½ inches thick
2 tablespoons bottled steak
    sauce

Cook garlic in oil; remove from heat. Add wine, lemon juice, basil, dry mustard, and ½ teaspoon salt. Prick roast on both sides with long-tined fork; place in plastic bag and set in deep bowl. Pour in marinade; close bag. Marinate overnight in refrigerator, turning roast in bag or pressing marinade against roast occasionally. Drain meat, reserving marinade. Remove excess moisture from roast with paper toweling. Add steak sauce to reserved marinade. Grill over *medium* coals 25 to 30 minutes on each side for medium doneness. Brush with marinade. Serves 6 to 8.

Avoid Flair-Ups with a Drip Pan

When grilling large pieces of meat, use a drip pan to catch meat juices. Make your own pan as follows: (A) Tear off a piece of 18-inch-wide heavy-duty foil twice the length of your grill and fold it in half for a double thickness. Turn up all edges of the foil 1½ inches. (B) Miter corners securely and fold tips toward the inside for added strength. (C) Set the drip pan under the meat to catch drippings, and arrange the coals around the pan. Position the pan in place either before or after you ignite the charcoal. Carefully empty the drip pan after each use.

HORSERADISH-STUFFED RUMP ROAST

¼ cup prepared horseradish
2 cloves garlic, minced
1 5-pound boneless beef rump
    roast, rolled and tied
1 clove garlic, halved

Combine horseradish and minced garlic. Unroll roast;
make a lengthwise cut slightly off-center going almost
to but not through other side. (Leave center area un-
cut for spit to go through.) Spread cut area with
horseradish mixture. Reroll roast and tie securely.
Insert spit rod through center of roast. Adjust holding
forks; test balance. Rub outside of roast with the additional clove of garlic. Insert meat thermometer. Place
medium coals on both sides of drip pan. Attach spit;
position drip pan under meat. Turn on motor; lower
hood or cover with foil tent. Roast till thermometer
registers 140° for medium-rare, about 1½ hours. Let
stand 15 minutes before carving. Serves 10.

WINE-BASTED SHORT RIBS

½ cup dry red wine
1 teaspoon dried thyme, crushed
½ teaspoon garlic salt
½ teaspoon lemon pepper
2 pounds beef plate short ribs,
    cut in serving-size pieces

In large Dutch oven combine wine, thyme, garlic salt,
lemon pepper, and ½ cup water. Add rib pieces. Cover
and simmer just till tender, 1¼ to 1½ hours. Drain, reserving liquid. Place ribs over *slow* coals. Grill till
done, 15 to 20 minutes, turning ribs occasionally and
brushing with wine mixture. Makes 4 servings.

SMOKED SHORT RIBS

Hickory chips
4 pounds beef plate short ribs,
    cut in serving-size pieces
1 10¾-ounce can condensed
    tomato soup
¾ cup dry red wine
¼ cup finely chopped onion
2 tablespoons cooking oil
1 tablespoon prepared mustard
2 teaspoons chili powder
1 teaspoon paprika
1 teaspoon celery seed
¼ teaspoon salt

Soak hickory chips in enough water to cover about an hour before cooking time. Drain chips. In covered grill place *slow* coals on both sides of drip pan. Sprinkle coals with some dampened hickory chips. Place ribs, bone side down, on grill. Lower grill hood. Grill ribs till done, about 1½ hours, adding more hickory chips every 20 minutes.

Meanwhile, in saucepan mix tomato soup, wine, onion, cooking oil, mustard, chili powder, paprika, celery seed, and ¼ teaspoon salt. Heat sauce at side of grill. Brush ribs with sauce. Grill, uncovered, about 20 minutes more; brush ribs frequently with sauce. Serves 4 or 5.

*Be Sure with
a Meat
Thermometer*

Using a meat thermometer helps you make sure your roasts are cooked the way you want them— to perfection. Insert thermometer in center of raw roast so tip reaches thickest part of meat and does not touch fat, bone, or metal spit rod. When thermometer registers the doneness you like (see charts, pages 2–5), push it into meat a little farther. If temperature drops below the desired temperature, continue cooking till it rises again.

QUICK GARLIC CUBED STEAKS

¼ cup butter *or* margarine
2 tablespoons Worcestershire
    sauce
2 tablespoons lemon juice
1 teaspoon finely snipped
    parsley
½ teaspoon celery salt
1 clove garlic, minced
6 beef cubed steaks
6 Vienna *or* French bread slices,
    toasted

In saucepan melt butter or margarine; stir in Worcestershire sauce, lemon juice, snipped parsley, celery salt, and garlic. Brush butter mixture on both sides of steaks. Place the steaks in wire grill basket. Grill over *hot* coals for 1 to 2 minutes. Turn basket over and grill for 1 to 2 minutes more. Season steaks with salt and pepper. Place each steak atop a slice of toasted bread. Spoon remaining butter mixture over steaks. Serves 6.

BEEF AND BEAN RAGOUT

2 tablespoons cooking oil
2 pounds beef for stew, cut
   in ½-inch pieces
3½ cups water
3 medium potatoes, peeled and
   cubed (3 cups)
2 cups chopped peeled
   tomatoes *or* 1 16-ounce can
   tomatoes, cut up
2 medium onions, chopped
1 6-ounce can tomato paste
1 medium green pepper, chopped
¼ cup snipped parsley
1 tablespoon instant beef
   bouillon granules
1½ teaspoons salt
1 teaspoon sugar
½ teaspoon dried basil,
   crushed
½ teaspoon dried thyme,
   crushed
¼ teaspoon pepper
1 bay leaf
1 15½-ounce can red kidney
   beans, drained
¼ cup dry red wine
¼ cup all-purpose flour

Heat oil in heavy 4-quart Dutch over over *hot* coals;
brown half the meat at a time in the hot oil. Add 3
cups of the water, potatoes, tomatoes, onions, tomato
paste, green pepper, parsley, beef bouillon granules,
and seasonings. Cover and heat to boiling (will take
about 1¼ hours), stirring occasionally. Add coals as
necessary. Boil till meat and vegetables are tender,
about 1 hour more, stirring occasionally. Stir in beans
and wine. Cover and heat to boiling. Blend the re-

maining ½ cup water into the flour; stir into bean mixture. Cook, stirring constantly, till mixture thickens and bubbles. Remove bay leaf. Makes 6 servings.

SMOKED BEEF AND CHEESE SOUP

    4 cups milk
    1 10¾-ounce can cream of
        potato soup
    1 4-ounce package sliced smoked
        beef, snipped (1 cup)
    1 cup shredded Muenster cheese
    ¼ cup finely chopped onion
    2 tablespoons snipped parsley
    ½ teaspoon caraway seed

In heavy 3-quart saucepan gradually stir milk into soup. Add smoked beef, cheese, onion, parsley, and caraway seed. Cook and stir over *hot* coals till mixture is heated through, about 30 minutes, stirring often. Serves 6 to 8.

BEEF AND MUSHROOM KABOBS

    ½ cup cooking oil
    ⅓ cup soy sauce
    ¼ cup lemon juice
    2 tablespoons prepared
        mustard
    2 tablespoons Worcestershire
        sauce
    1 clove garlic, minced
    1 teaspoon coarsely cracked
        pepper
    1½ teaspoons salt
    1½ pounds lean beef round *or*
        chuck, cut in 1-inch pieces
    Boiling water
    12 to 16 mushroom caps

Mix oil, soy sauce, lemon juice, mustard, Worcestershire, garlic, pepper, and 1½ teaspoons salt. Add beef pieces. Cover and refrigerate overnight; turn meat occasionally. Pour boiling water over mushrooms. Let stand a few minutes; drain. Thread meat and mushrooms on skewers. Grill over *hot* coals till meat is desired doneness; allow 15 minutes for medium-rare; turn often. Makes 4 or 5 servings.

STEAK AND SHRIMP KABOB DINNER

½ cup catsup
¼ cup water
¼ cup finely chopped onion
1 tablespoon brown sugar
3 tablespoons lemon juice
2 tablespoons cooking oil
2 teaspoons prepared mustard
2 teaspoons Worcestershire
   sauce
½ teaspoon chili powder
1 pound beef sirloin steak, cut
   in 1-inch pieces
½ pound fresh *or* frozen shrimp,
   shelled
2 zucchini, cut diagonally in
   1-inch pieces
2 ears corn, cut in 1-inch pieces
2 small onions, cut in wedges
1 green pepper *or* red sweet
   pepper, cut in squares
6 cherry tomatoes

In small saucepan combine catsup, water, chopped onion, and brown sugar. Stir in lemon juice, cooking oil, prepared mustard, Worcestershire sauce, and chili powder. Simmer, uncovered, 10 minutes, stirring once or twice.

On six short skewers thread steak pieces alternately

with shrimp, zucchini, corn, onion wedges, and pepper squares. Grill kabobs over *medium-hot* coals till meat is desired doneness, allow 15 to 17 minutes for medium-rare. Turn kabobs often, brushing with sauce. Garnish end of each skewer with a cherry tomato. Makes 3 or 4 servings.

How to Turn Barbecued Steaks

Every time a drop of meat juice falls to its sizzling end on the coals, you're losing a little bit of the flavor that makes barbecued steak so delicious. To prevent this flavor loss, be sure to use tongs when turning the meat. Or, if you don't have tongs, insert a fork into a strip of fat and flip steak with a turner.

BEEF-YAM KABOBS

4 medium yams *or* sweet potatoes
    or 1 8-ounce can syrup-
    packed sweet potatoes
¼ cup packed brown sugar
1 teaspoon cornstarch
½ cup orange juice
¼ cup chili sauce
1 tablespoon prepared mustard
1 pound beef sirloin steak, cut
    ½ inch thick
1 orange, cut into 8 wedges

Cut off woody portion of fresh yams or sweet potatoes. In saucepan cook fresh yams or sweet potatoes, covered, in enough boiling salted water to cover till potatoes are tender, 25 to 30 minutes. Drain; cool potatoes. Peel and cut into 1-inch pieces. (If using canned sweet potatoes, drain; cut sweet potatoes into 1-inch pieces.)

Meanwhile, prepare sauce. In small saucepan stir together brown sugar and cornstarch; stir in orange juice, chili sauce, and mustard. Cook, stirring constantly, till thickened and bubbly. Simmer, uncovered, 5 minutes; stirring once or twice. Sprinkle steak with salt and pepper; cut steak into 1-inch pieces. On four skewers alternately thread steak pieces, yam or sweet potato pieces, and orange wedges. Grill over *medium* coals till meat is desired doneness, allow 12 to 14 minutes for medium-rare. Turn kabobs occasionally and brush frequently with some of the sauce; pass remaining sauce. Makes 4 servings.

SKEWERED BEEF BUNDLES

⅓ cup soy sauce
2 tablespoons sugar
¼ teaspoon ground ginger
1 pound beef round tip steak,
    cut 1 inch thick
½ pound fresh whole green beans
4 large carrots, cut into
    3-inch-long sticks
2 tablespoons butter *or*
    margarine, melted

In medium bowl combine soy sauce, sugar, and ginger. Cut steak into thin strips. Cover; marinate meat in soy mixture for 2 to 3 hours at room temperature, stirring occasionally. Meanwhile, cook beans and carrots separately in boiling salted water till barely tender; drain well and cool. Wrap half the meat strips around bundles of four beans; repeat with remaining meat and carrot sticks. Secure with wooden picks. Thread bundles ladder fashion on two parallel skewers. Brush with melted butter. Grill over *medium* coals about 4 minutes. Turn and grill for 3 to 4 minutes more. Brush with melted butter once or twice more during cooking. Serves 4 or 5.

SKEWERED CHERRY TOMATO MEATBALLS

1 beaten egg
¾ cup soft bread crumbs
    (1 slice)
¼ cup milk
¼ cup finely chopped onion
¾ teaspoon salt
½ teaspoon dried oregano,
    crushed
⅛ teaspoon pepper
1 pound ground beef
15 cherry tomatoes
2 dill pickles, cut into
    ½-inch chunks
    Bottled steak sauce

In bowl combine egg, bread crumbs, milk, onion, salt, oregano, and pepper. Add ground beef; mix well. Shape 3 tablespoons of the meat mixture around each cherry tomato to form meatballs. On five large skewers thread meatballs and dill pickle chunks. Grill over *medium* coals for 15 to 20 minutes, turning 3 or 4 times to cook evenly; brush meatballs occasionally with steak sauce. Makes 5 servings.

HAWAIIAN KABOBS

½ cup soy sauce
¼ cup cooking oil
1 tablespoon dark corn
    syrup
2 cloves garlic, minced
1 teaspoon dry mustard
1 teaspoon ground ginger
2½ pounds beef sirloin steak, cut
    in 1½-inch pieces
3 green peppers, cut in
    1-inch squares
5 small firm tomatoes,
    quartered

In large bowl combine soy sauce, oil, corn syrup, garlic, dry mustard, and ginger. Add meat; cover and refrigerate several hours or overnight. Drain meat, reserving marinade. Alternate meat, green pepper, and tomato on skewers. Grill over *medium-hot* coals till desired doneness, allow about 15 minutes for rare. Baste the kabobs occasionally with reserved marinade. Makes 8 servings.

Burgers and Sandwiches

BURGERS O'BRIEN

1 12-ounce package frozen
   loose-pack hash brown
   potatoes (3 cups)
¼ cup chopped onion
¼ cup chopped green pepper
2 tablespoons melted butter
1 beaten egg
2 tablespoons chopped pimiento
1½ teaspoons salt
¼ teaspoon pepper
1½ pounds ground beef
8 hamburger buns, split,
   toasted, and buttered

Chop potatoes slightly; sprinkle with salt. In skillet combine potatoes, onion, green pepper, and butter. Cover and cook till potatoes are tender, stirring occasionally. Combine egg, pimiento, 1½ teaspoons salt, and pepper; stir in potato mixture. Add ground beef; mix well. Shape meat mixture into 8 patties, about ½ inch thick. Grill over *medium-hot* coals for 5 minutes. Turn and grill 3 to 4 minutes more. Serve patties on toasted buns; place green pepper ring atop burger, if desired. Serves 8.

BEEF AND CARROT BURGERS

1 beaten egg
2 tablespoons milk
¼ cup wheat germ
½ cup grated carrot
¼ cup finely chopped onion
¾ teaspoon salt
¼ teaspoon dried marjoram,
    crushed
⅛ teaspoon pepper
1 pound ground beef
4 slices Monterey Jack cheese
4 whole wheat hamburger buns,
    split, toasted, and buttered
4 lettuce leaves
4 tomato slices

Combine egg, milk, and wheat germ; stir in carrot, onion, salt, marjoram, and pepper. Add ground beef; mix well. Shape into four patties. Grill over *medium-hot* coals for 5 to 6 minutes; turn and grill 4 to 5 minutes more. During last minute of cooking time, place a slice of cheese atop each patty. Serve patties on toasted buns with lettuce and tomato. Makes 4 servings.

BURGERS EXTRAVAGANZA

    1 beaten egg
    ¼ cup water
    ¼ cup fine dry bread crumbs
    ¼ teaspoon dried oregano,
        crushed
    ¼ teaspoon fennel seed
    ¼ teaspoon garlic salt
    ¼ teaspoon onion salt
      Dash pepper
  1½ pounds ground beef
    ½ pound bulk pork sausage
    8 slices American cheese
    8 onion slices
    8 hamburger buns, split,
        toasted, and buttered

In bowl combine egg, water, bread crumbs, oregano,
fennel, garlic salt, onion salt, and pepper. Add ground
beef and sausage; mix well. Form into 8 patties, ½ inch
thick. Grill burgers over *medium* coals for 6 to 7 minutes. Turn and cook 6 to 7 minutes more. Top each
patty with a cheese and onion slice; serve on toasted
buns. Makes 8 servings.

BACON BURGER SQUARES

    8 slices bacon
    2 pounds ground beef
    2 tablespoons lemon juice
    1 tablespoon Worcestershire
        sauce
      Salt
      Pepper
    8 hamburger buns, split and
        toasted

Cook bacon till almost done, but not crisp. Cut bacon strips in half crosswise. Pat ground beef to a 12x6-inch rectangle; cut into 8 squares. Combine lemon juice and Worcestershire; brush over the beef patties. Sprinkle with salt and pepper. Arrange squares in greased wire grill basket. Place 2 half-slices of bacon crisscrossed atop each burger to form an "X." Close basket. Grill burgers over *medium-hot* coals, turning often, till desired doneness, about 20 minutes. Serve on hamburger buns. Serves 8.

CHILI BURGER PATTIES

2½ pounds ground beef
¾ cup chili sauce
4 teaspoons prepared mustard
4 teaspoons prepared horseradish
4 teaspoons Worcestershire sauce
1 tablespoon chopped onion
2 teaspoons salt
  Dash pepper
12 hamburger buns, split
   and toasted

In mixing bowl thoroughly combine ground beef, chili sauce, prepared mustard, horseradish, Worcestershire sauce, chopped onion, salt, and pepper; mix well. Form into 12 patties. Grill over *medium-hot* coals for 5 minutes. Turn patties and grill till desired doneness, about 3 minutes longer. Serve grilled patties on hamburger buns. Serves 12.

BASIC GRILLED BURGERS

1 pound ground beef
½ teaspoon salt
  Dash pepper

Mix ground beef, salt, and pepper. Form into four 4-inch patties. Grill over *medium-hot* coals for 5 to 6 minutes; turn and grill 4 to 5 minutes more. Serves 4.

For Variations: Add any of the following to basic meat mixture; 2 tablespoons chopped green onion with tops; 2 tablespoons drained sweet pickle relish; 2 tablespoons chopped pimiento-stuffed olives; 1 tablespoon prepared horseradish; or ¼ teaspoon instant minced garlic.

BARBECUED BEEF BURGERS

1 beaten egg
2 tablespoons milk
2 tablespoons catsup
¼ cup finely crushed saltine
    crackers (7 crackers)
½ teaspoon salt
1 pound ground beef
4 thin slices onion
4 slices sharp American cheese
¼ cup chopped onion
¼ cup butter *or* margarine
¼ cup catsup
2 tablespoons brown sugar
½ teaspoon prepared horseradish
½ teaspoon salt

Combine egg, milk, and 2 tablespoons catsup; stir in cracker crumbs and ½ teaspoon salt. Add ground beef; mix well. Form into four patties; place each on a 12-inch square of heavy-duty foil. Top each patty with 1 slice onion and 1 slice cheese.

Cook chopped onion in butter till tender but not brown. Add ¼ cup catsup, brown sugar, horseradish, and ½ teaspoon salt; simmer, uncovered, 5 minutes. Spoon over burgers. Wrap foil loosely around meat, sealing edges well. Cook the bundles over *medium* coals, onion side down, for 15 minutes. Turn burgers over; grill till desired doneness, about 10 minutes more. Makes 4 servings.

VEGETABLE BURGERS

   2 slightly beaten eggs
   ¾ cup soft bread crumbs
   ¼ cup finely chopped onion
   ¼ cup catsup
 1½ pounds ground beef
   1 6-ounce can chopped
       mushrooms, drained
   6 slices American cheese
   6 hamburger buns
   6 slices onion
   6 slices tomato

In bowl combine eggs, crumbs, onion, catsup, 1 teaspoon salt, and dash pepper. Add beef; mix well. Form into 12 patties. Top *half* of the patties with mushrooms to within ¼ inch of edge. Top with remaining patties, sealing edges. Grill over *medium* coals for 5 to 6 minutes. Turn and grill till desired doneness, 5 to 6 minutes more. Top with cheese; heat just till melted. Split and toast hamburger buns. Serve burgers on buns with onion and tomato slices. Makes 6 servings.

CHEESE-STUFFED PATTIES

   1 pound ground beef
   ½ teaspoon salt
    Dash pepper
    American cheese, shredded
    Chopped onion
    Bottled barbecue sauce

Mix ground beef, salt, and pepper. Between sheets of waxed paper, roll out patties ¼ inch thick. Center half

of patties with small amount of cheese, onion, and barbecue sauce. Top with remaining meat patties; press
around edges to seal. Grill over *medium-hot* coals
about 7 minutes. Turn meat; grill 6 to 7 minutes more.
Makes 3 burgers.

BURRITO BURGERS

  1 cup refried beans
     (½ of 15-ounce can)
  1 4-ounce can mild green chili
     peppers, drained, seeded,
     and chopped
  ¼ cup chopped onion
1½ pounds ground beef
  4 slices sharp American cheese
  8 flour tortillas
  1 cup chopped lettuce
  1 medium tomato, chopped

Combine beans, 2 *tablespoons* of the chili peppers,
onion, and ¾ teaspoon salt. Add beef; mix well. Form
into eight 5-inch patties. Cut cheese slices in half;
place ½ cheese slice on each beef patty. Fold to seal
cheese inside, forming semicircle. Grill over *medium*
coals for 5 to 6 minutes; turn and grill 4 to 5 minutes
more. Heat the tortillas on grill. Serve burgers in hot
tortillas. Add the lettuce, chopped tomato, and remaining chili peppers as desired. Makes 8 servings.

> ### Don't Do
> ### without a Wire
> ### Grill Basket
>
> Wire grill baskets are indispensable when you grill foods that need frequent turning or are difficult to turn, such as burgers, frankfurters, bite-size rib appetizers, chops, or shrimp. A hinged grill basket is the best buy, since you can adjust it to hold small fish, thick burgers, thin steaks, or chicken halves, quarters, or cut-up pieces.

MINI PINEAPPLE MEAT LOAVES

- 1 15¼-ounce can crushed
    pineapple (juice pack)
- 2 beaten eggs
- 1½ cups soft bread crumbs
    (2 slices)
- 2 tablespoons finely chopped
    onion
- 2 tablespoons chopped green
    pepper
- ½ teaspoon salt
- ⅛ teaspoon pepper
- 1½ pounds ground beef
- 1 tablespoon cornstarch
- 2 teaspoons prepared mustard
- ¼ cup catsup
- 2 tablespoons soy sauce
- 4 drops bottled hot pepper sauce

Drain crushed pineapple; reserve juice. Add water to juice, if necessary, to make 1 cup; set aside for use in sauce. In bowl combine eggs, bread crumbs, pineapple, onion, green pepper, salt, and pepper. Add beef; mix well. Form into five 4x2-inch loaves. Place meat loaves in wire grill basket. Grill over *medium-*

hot coals for 20 to 25 minutes. Turn and grill till done, about 20 minutes more.

Meanwhile, in small saucepan blend together cornstarch and mustard. Stir in reserved pineapple juice, catsup, soy sauce, and hot pepper sauce. Cook over *medium-hot* coals, stirring constantly, till thickened and bubbly. Pass with the meat loaves. Makes 5 servings.

GIANT STUFFED GRILLBURGERS

1 beaten egg
1¼ cup herb-seasoned
    stuffing mix, crushed
1 4-ounce can chopped
    mushrooms, drained
⅓ cup beef broth
¼ cup sliced green onion
    with tops
¼ cup snipped parsley
2 tablespoons butter *or*
    margarine, melted
1 teaspoon lemon juice
2 pounds ground beef
1 teaspoon salt

Mix together the egg, stuffing mix, drained mushrooms, beef broth, green onion, parsley, butter or margarine, and lemon juice; set aside. Combine meat and salt; divide mixture in half. On sheets of waxed paper, pat each half to an 8-inch circle. Spoon stuffing over one circle of meat to within 1 inch of edge. Top with second circle of meat; peel off top sheet of paper and seal edges of meat.

Invert meat patty onto well-greased wire grill basket; peel off remaining paper. Grill over *medium* coals for 10 to 12 minutes. Turn and grill till desired doneness, 10 to 12 minutes more. Cut the burger into wedges; serve with warmed catsup, if desired. Makes 8 servings.

CHILI MEAT LOAF

2 slightly beaten eggs
1 8-ounce can tomatoes, cut up
1 8-ounce can red kidney beans,
   drained
1 cup crushed corn chips
¼ cup finely chopped green onion
   with tops
2 tablespoons snipped parsley
1½ teaspoons salt
1 teaspoon chili powder
2 pounds lean ground beef
1 10-ounce can mild enchilada
   sauce
½ cup shredded sharp American
   cheese (2 ounces)

Combine eggs, undrained tomatoes, beans, corn chips, green onion, parsley, salt, and chili powder; mash beans slightly. Add ground beef; mix well. Shape into two 7x3x2-inch loaves. Tear off two 18-inch lengths of 18-inch-wide heavy-duty foil. Place loaves on foil pieces; wrap foil around each loaf and seal securely. Grill over *medium* coals 30 minutes. Turn and grill 20 minutes longer.

Meanwhile, in saucepan heat enchilada sauce. Open foil and fold down to make "pan." Continue cooking meat till done, about 10 minutes more, brushing frequently with enchilada sauce. Pass remaining sauce and cheese to top each serving. Makes 8 servings.

STUFFED STEAK SANDWICHES

   2 1-pound beef flank steaks
     Instant unseasoned meat
       tenderizer
   2 tablespoons prepared
       horseradish
   ⅛ cup chopped onion
   ⅛ cup chopped celery
   2 tablespoons butter *or*
       margarine, melted
   ½ teaspoon seasoned salt
   1 cup dairy sour cream
  12 slices French bread, toasted
       and buttered

Score steaks diagonally on both sides. Use tenderizer
according to directions. Spread one side of steaks with
horseradish. Combine onion, celery, butter, and seasoned salt; spread on steaks. Roll up as for jelly roll.
Fasten with skewers and tie with string. Insert spit rod
through center of meat rolls. Adjust holding forks;
test balance. Place *medium* coals on both sides of drip
pan. Attach spit; position drip pan under meat. Turn
on motor. Grill over *medium* coals till done, about 45
minutes. Let stand a few minutes; remove strings and
skewers.

   In small saucepan heat sour cream over low heat; *do
not boil*. Carefully carve meat rolls into thin slices and
place on bread. Spoon warm sour cream atop meat.
Serves 6.

PIZZA-FRANK SANDWICHES

1 beaten egg
¼ cup milk
¾ cup soft bread crumbs
¼ cup grated Parmesan cheese
2 tablespoons snipped parsley
½ teaspoon garlic salt
  Dash pepper
½ pound bulk pizza sausage
½ pound ground beef
6 frankfurters
1 8-ounce can pizza sauce
2 tablespoons chopped onion
2 tablespoons sliced pimiento-
    stuffed green olives
6 frankfurter buns, split and
    toasted
⅓ cup shredded mozzarella
    cheese

Combine egg and milk; stir in crumbs, Parmesan cheese, parsley, garlic salt, and pepper. Add sausage and beef; mix thoroughly. Divide into 6 equal portions. Shape meat around frankfurters, leaving ends open; roll each between waxed paper to make uniform thickness. Chill.

In saucepan combine pizza sauce, chopped onion, and green olives. Simmer, uncovered, 5 minutes; stir occasionally. Grill frankfurters over *medium* coals till meat is set, about 5 minutes. Turn and grill till meat is done, about 10 minutes more. Brush with pizza sauce mixture during the last five minutes. Serve on toasted buns. Spoon remaining pizza sauce atop sandwiches and sprinkle with shredded mozzarella cheese. Makes 6 servings.

SPICED HAM PATTIES

1 slightly beaten egg
¼ cup milk
1½ cups soft bread crumbs
    (2 slices bread)
1 tablespoon finely chopped
    green onion with tops
  Dash pepper
1 pound ground cooked ham
    (3 cups)
⅓ cup packed brown sugar
¼ cup honey
1 teaspoon dry mustard
¼ cup reserved spiced apple
    syrup
4 spiced apple rings

Combine the egg and milk; stir in bread crumbs, onion, and pepper. Add ham; mix well. Shape mixture into four 4-inch patties. In saucepan combine brown sugar, honey, dry mustard, and the spiced apple syrup; heat through. Grill patties over *medium-hot* coals for 5 minutes. Turn; brush with glaze. Place an apple ring atop each patty; brush with glaze. Grill ham patties till done, 5 to 6 minutes more. Pass remaining glaze with patties. Serves 4.

CORNED BEEF–TURKEY HEROES

8 Kaiser rolls *or* hamburger
    buns, split
Tartar sauce
Russian, Italian, *or* blue
    cheese salad dressing
2 3- or 4-ounce packages thinly
    sliced smoked corned beef
8 thin onion slices
4 slices Swiss cheese,
    cut in half
2 3- or 4-ounce packages thinly
    sliced smoked turkey

Lightly spread cut surfaces of Kaiser rolls or buns with tartar sauce and salad dressing. Layer slices of the corned beef, onion, Swiss cheese, and turkey on rolls. Replace tops of rolls; place each sandwich on an 18x12-inch rectangle of heavy-duty foil. Wrap foil around sandwiches, sealing edges well. Grill over *medium* coals till heated through, about 25 minutes, turning several times. Serves 8.

BRATWURSTS IN BEER

1 12-ounce can beer (1½ cups)
2 tablespoons brown sugar
2 tablespoons soy sauce
1 tablespoon prepared mustard
1 teaspoon chili powder
2 cloves garlic, minced
Several drops hot pepper sauce
6 bratwursts
6 individual French rolls
Zesty Sauerkraut Relish
    (see recipe, page 116)

Combine beer, brown sugar, soy sauce, mustard, chili powder, garlic, and hot pepper sauce. Place brats in shallow baking dish; pour marinade over. Cover; refrigerate several hours or overnight, spooning marinade over occasionally. Remove brats, reserving marinade. Grill over *medium-hot* coals about 4 minutes. Turn and grill till done, 3 to 4 minutes more. Brush often with reserved marinade. Cut rolls in half lengthwise; hollow out rolls, leaving a ¼-inch wall. Fill each roll bottom with about ¼ cup drained relish. Add bratwurst and top with roll top. (Refrigerate remaining relish until needed.) Makes 6 servings.

ORIENTAL PORK WRAP-UPS

3 tablespoons chopped green
    onion with tops
4 teaspoons soy sauce
⅛ teaspoon garlic powder
1 pound ground pork
    Sweet-Sour Sauce
8 leaf lettuce leaves *or*
    lettuce cups
    Parsley Rice

Combine green onion, soy sauce, and garlic powder. Add ground pork; mix well. Shape mixture into eight 3x1-inch logs. Grill over *medium* coals for 4 to 5 minutes; turn and brush with Sweet-Sour Sauce. Grill logs till done, 3 to 4 minutes more. In center of each leaf lettuce place about 1 tablespoon Parsley Rice. Place a grilled log horizontally atop rice. Fold two opposite edges of lettuce crosswise so they overlap atop logs. Dip the bundle in Sweet-Sour Sauce for each bite. (Or, place rice in lettuce cups; top with pork log. Drizzle sauce over.) Serves 4.

Sweet-Sour Sauce: In saucepan combine ½ cup packed brown sugar and 1 tablespoon cornstarch. Stir in ⅛ cup red wine vinegar, ⅛ cup chicken broth, ¼ cup finely chopped green pepper, 2 tablespoons chopped pimiento, 1 tablespoon soy sauce, ¼ teaspoon garlic powder, and ¼ teaspoon ground ginger. Place over *medium* coals, stirring occasionally, till thickened and bubbly. Makes 1¼ cups sauce.

Parsley Rice: In saucepan combine ⅔ cup water, ⅓ cup regular rice, and ¼ teaspoon salt. Cover with tight-fitting lid. Bring to boiling over *medium* coals, about 15 minutes. Move to edge of coals; cook 10 minutes more (do not lift cover). Remove from heat; let stand, covered, 10 minutes. Stir in 2 tablespoons snipped parsley.

GRILLED CRAB AND CHEESE ROLLS

1 cup shredded Monterey Jack
    cheese (4 ounces)
¼ cup finely chopped celery
2 tablespoons mayonnaise *or*
    salad dressing
2 tablespoons chopped pimiento
2 teaspoons lemon juice
1 teaspoon prepared mustard
1 7½-ounce can crab meat,
    drained, flaked, and
    cartilage removed
4 individual French rolls

Stir together cheese, celery, mayonnaise or salad dressing, pimiento, lemon juice, and prepared mustard. Fold in crab. Split French rolls; spread crab mixture over bottom halves and replace tops. Wrap heavy-duty foil loosely around roll; fold edges of foil to seal tightly. Grill over *medium* coals for 10 minutes. Turn; grill till heated through, about 10 minutes more. Makes 4 servings.

Pork and Ham

APPLE-ORANGE STUFFED PORK CHOPS

6 pork loin chops, cut
 1½ inches thick
½ cup chopped celery
½ cup chopped unpeeled apple
 (1 medium)
2 tablespoons butter
1 beaten egg
1½ cups toasted raisin bread
 cubes (2½ slices)
½ teaspoon grated orange peel
1 orange, sectioned and chopped
 (⅓ cup)
¼ teaspoon salt
⅛ teaspoon ground cinnamon

Make a slit in each chop by cutting from fat side almost to bone. Season cavity with a little salt and pepper.

In small saucepan cook celery and apple in butter till tender but not brown. Combine egg, bread cubes, orange peel, chopped orange, salt, and cinnamon. Pour cooked celery and apple over bread cube mixture; toss lightly. Spoon about ¼ cup stuffing into each pork chop. Securely fasten pocket opening with wooden picks.

Grill chops over *medium* coals about 20 minutes. Turn meat and grill till done, 15 to 20 minutes more. Before serving remove the picks. Makes 6 servings.

CORN-STUFFED PORK CHOPS

    6 pork loin chops, cut
         1½ inches thick
    ¼ cup chopped green pepper
    ¼ cup chopped onion
    1 tablespoon butter *or*
         margarine
    1 beaten egg
    1½ cups toasted bread cubes
    ½ cup cooked whole kernel corn
    2 tablespoons chopped pimiento
    ½ teaspoon salt
    ¼ teaspoon ground cumin
         Dash pepper

Make a slit in each chop by cutting from fat side almost to bone. Season cavity with a little salt and pepper.

In small saucepan cook green pepper and onion in butter till tender but not brown. Combine egg, bread cubes, corn, pimiento, salt, cumin, and pepper. Pour cooked pepper and onion over bread cube mixture; toss lightly. Spoon about ¼ cup stuffing into each pork chop. Securely fasten pocket opening with wooden picks.

Grill chops over *medium* coals about 20 minutes. Turn meat and grill till done, 15 to 20 minutes more. Before serving, remove the picks. Makes 6 servings.

ROAST PORK CHOPS

1 cup chopped onion
1 clove garlic, minced
2 tablespoons cooking oil
¾ cup catsup
¼ cup lemon juice
3 tablespoons sugar
2 tablespoons Worcestershire
    sauce
1 tablespoon prepared mustard
1 teaspoon salt
¼ teaspoon bottled hot pepper
    sauce
  Salt
6 pork loin chops *or* rib chops,
    cut 1¼ to 1½ inches thick

In saucepan cook onion and garlic in hot oil till tender but not brown. Stir in catsup, lemon juice, sugar, Worcestershire sauce, prapared mustard, 1 teaspoon salt, and bottled hot pepper sauce. Simmer, uncovered, 5 minutes, stirring once or twice. Sprinkle chops with salt.

Place chops in wire grill basket. Grill chops over *medium* coals about 25 minutes. Turn meat and grill about 20 minutes more, brushing with sauce occasionally. Serves 6.

GYPSY PORK STEAKS

2 whole pork tenderloins
    (1½ pounds)
4 teaspoons paprika
1 teaspoon salt
⅛ teaspoon pepper

Cut tenderloin into six 3-inch pieces. Resting each piece on cut side, flatten with side of cleaver or meat mallet to ¾-inch thickness. Stir together paprika, salt, and pepper. Coat meat on both sides with seasoning mixture. Grill pork over *medium* coals about 10 minutes. Turn meat and grill till done, about 10 minutes more. Serves 6.

APPLE–PEANUT BUTTERED PORK STEAKS

½ cup apple butter
2 tablespoons peanut butter
¼ teaspoon finely shredded
    orange peel
2 tablespoons orange juice
4 pork blade steaks,
    cut ¾ inch thick

Blend apple butter into peanut butter; add orange peel and juice. Season steaks with salt and pepper. Grill over *medium* coals for about 15 minutes. Turn steaks; brush with apple butter mixture. Grill till done, 15 to 20 minutes more. Brush on remaining apple butter mixture. Serves 4.

Note: If desired, use 1½-inch-thick steaks. Grill 25 minutes. Turn; grill till done, about 25 minutes. Serves 8.

MARINATED PORK LOIN ROAST

1 5-pound boneless pork loin
    roast, rolled and tied
¼ cup water
3 tablespoons Dijon-style mustard
2 tablespoons cooking oil
1 tablespoon soy sauce

Pierce pork loin in several places wiht long-tined fork; place in shallow baking dish. Blend water, mustard, oil, and soy; brush over meat. Cover; let stand at room temperature 1 hour. Drain meat; reserve sauce. Insert spit rod through center of roast. Adjust holding forks; test balance. Insert meat thermometer near center of roast, not touching rod. Place *medium-hot* coals on both sides of drip pan. Attach spit; position drip pan under meat. Turn on motor. Grill till thermometer registers 170° for well-done, 2 to 2½ hours.

During last 30 to 45 minutes, brush meat with mustard sauce. Heat remaining sauce; pass with meat. Serves 8.

COMPANY PORK LOIN ROAST

1 cup catsup
¼ cup cooking oil
¼ cup wine vinegar
2 tablespoons instant minced
   onion
2 tablespoons Worcestershire
   sauce
1 tablespoon brown sugar
1 teaspoon mustard seed
1 teaspoon dried oregano,
   crushed
1 bay leaf
½ teaspoon salt
½ teaspoon cracked pepper
¼ teaspoon chili powder
1 5-pound boneless pork loin
   roast, rolled and tied

In saucepan combine catsup, cooking oil, wine vinegar, onion. Worcestershire sauce, brown sugar, mustard seed, oregano, bay leaf, salt, pepper, chili powder, and ½ cup water. Simmer the mixture 20 minutes; remove bay leaf.

Insert spit rod through center of roast. Adjust holding forks and test balance. Insert meat thermometer near center of roast, not touching spit rod. In covered grill place *medium-hot* coals on both sides of drip pan. Attach spit; position drip pan under meat. Turn on motor; lower grill hood or cover with foil tent. Grill till meat thermometer registers 170° for well-done, 2 to 2½ hours. Brush with sauce frequently during last 30 minutes. Serves 8.

HICKORY-SMOKED ROYAL RIBS

  Hickory chips
¾ cup catsup
½ cup finely chopped onion
¼ cup olive oil *or* cooking oil
¼ cup tarragon vinegar
¼ cup water
3 tablespoons lemon juice
2 tablespoons Worcestershire
  sauce
1 tablespoon brown sugar
2 teaspoons dry mustard
2 teaspoons paprika
2 teaspoons chili powder
2 cloves garlic, minced
2 bay leaves
1 teaspoon cumin seed, crushed
1 teaspoon dried thyme, crushed
½ teaspoon salt
¼ teaspoon pepper
4 pounds pork loin back ribs *or*
  spareribs

Soak hickory chips in enough water to cover for about 1 hour before cooking time; drain. In saucepan stir together catsup, onion, oil, vinegar, water, lemon juice. Worcestershire sauce, brown sugar, dry mustard, paprika, chili powder, garlic, bay leaves, cumin seed, thyme, salt, and pepper; simmer 10 minutes.

Lace ribs accordion-style on spit; secure with holding forks. In covered grill place *hot* coals on both sides of foil drip pan. Sprinkle coals with some dampened hickory chips. Attach spit; position drip pan under meat. Turn on motor; lower the grill hood or cover with foil tent. Grill the ribs over hot coals till done, about 1 hour. Sprinkle the coals with chips every 20 minutes. Brush ribs frequently with sauce mixture during the last 15 minutes of cooking. Pass the remaining sauce. Serves 4 to 6.

LUAU SPARERIBS

1 cup pineapple preserves
2 tablespoons vinegar
2 tablespoons chopped pimiento
1 tablespoon lemon juice
2 teaspoons Dijon-style mustard
1 teaspoon Kitchen Bouquet
3 to 4 pounds pork spareribs
    Salt
1 fresh pineapple, peeled and
    cut into lengthwise wedges
1 green pepper, cut into
    lengthwise strips

In a bowl combine the pineapple preserves, vinegar, pimiento, lemon juice, mustard, and Kitchen Bouquet; set aside.

Sprinkle the ribs with salt. Lace ribs, pineapple wedges, and green pepper strips accordion-style on spit; secure with holding forks. In covered grill place *slow* coals on both sides of foil drip pan. Attach spit; position drip pan under meat. Turn on motor; lower grill hood or cover with foil tent.

Grill the ribs over *slow* coals till done, about 1 hour. During the last 15 minutes of cooking time, brush the meat, pineapple wedges, and green pepper occasionally with the pineapple glaze. Makes 3 or 4 servings.

For smoke flavor sprinkle coals with dampened hickory chips during the last 30 minutes of cooking.

How to
Barbecue Ribs

If your grill has a spit attachment, try using it to barbecue long strips of pork spareribs or pork loin back ribs. Simply lace the ribs on the spit accordion-style. Secure the ribs with holding forks so they'll stay in position while rotating over the coals.

CHINESE SMOKED RIBS

6 pounds pork loin back ribs
    or spareribs
2 tablespoons sugar
1 teaspoon salt
½ teaspoon paprika
½ teaspoon ground turmeric
¼ teaspoon celery seed
⅛ teaspoon dry mustard
    Hickory chips
½ cup catsup
½ cup packed brown sugar
3 tablespoons soy sauce
1 tablespoon grated fresh
    gingerroot *or* 2 teaspoons
    ground ginger
1 clove garlic, minced

Thoroughly rub the ribs with mixture of sugar, salt, paprika, turmeric, celery seed, and dry mustard; cover and let stand 2 hours. About an hour before cooking time soak hickory chips in enough water to cover; drain.

In covered grill place *slow* coals on both sides of drip pan. Sprinkle coals with dampened hickory chips. Place ribs, bone side down, on grill; lower grill hood. Grill ribs over *slow* coals about 30 minutes. Turn meat and grill about 30 minutes more. Sprinkle coals with chips every 20 minutes. (If the thin end of spareribs cooks too quickly, place foil under thin end of ribs and continue cooking.)

Meanwhile, in saucepan combine catsup, brown sugar, soy sauce, ginger, and garlic. Cook and stir till sugar is dissolved. Brush mixture on both sides of ribs and grill, uncovered, till done, 10 to 15 minutes more. Heat any remaining sauce and serve with ribs. Makes 6 servings.

COUNTRY-STYLE BARBECUED RIBS

4 pounds pork country-style
  ribs
1 cup chopped onion
1 clove garlic, minced
¼ cup cooking oil
1 8-ounce can tomato sauce
½ cup water
¼ cup packed brown sugar
¼ cup lemon juice
2 tablespoons Worcestershire
  sauce
2 tablespoons prepared mustard
1 teaspoon salt
1 teaspoon celery seed
¼ teaspoon pepper

In large saucepan or Dutch oven cook ribs, covered, in enough boiling salted water to cover till ribs are tender, 45 to 60 minutes; drain well.

Meanwhile, in saucepan cook onion and garlic in hot oil till tender but not brown. Stir in tomato sauce, water, brown sugar, lemon juice, Worcestershire sauce, mustard, salt, celery seed, and pepper. Simmer, uncovered, 15 minutes; stir once or twice.

Grill ribs over *slow* coals till done, about 45 minutes, turning every 15 minutes. Brush with sauce till ribs are well coated. Makes 6 servings

APRICOT GLAZED RIBS

4 pounds pork loin back ribs,
  cut in serving-size pieces
1½ cup water
1 cup snipped dried apricots
½ cup packed brown sugar
2 tablespoons vinegar
1 tablespoon lemon juice
1 teaspoon ground ginger
½ teaspoon salt

In large saucepan or Dutch oven cook ribs, covered, in enough boiling salted water to cover till ribs are tender, 45 to 60 minutes. Drain well; season the ribs with a little salt and pepper.

Meanwhile, in a small saucepan combine the 1½ cups water, apricots, brown sugar, vinegar, lemon juice, ginger, and salt. Bring the mixture to boiling. Reduce heat; cover and simmer 5 minutes. Pour mixture into blender container. Cover and blend till smooth.

Brush the glaze over the ribs. Grill ribs over *medium-slow* coals for 10 to 15 minutes. Turn ribs and grill till done, 10 to 15 minutes more; brush occasionally with the apricot glaze. Makes 4 servings.

GLAZED PORK KABOBS

4 large carrots
½ cup apricot preserves
½ of an 8-ounce can tomato sauce
¼ cup packed brown sugar
¼ cup dry red wine
2 tablespoons lemon juice
2 tablespoons cooking oil
1 teaspoon onion juice
1½ pounds lean boneless pork
  Fresh pineapple chunks

Cut carrots into 1-inch pieces. In small saucepan cook, covered, in small amount boiling salted water for 15 to 20 minutes; drain. In saucepan combine apricot preserves, tomato sauce, brown sugar, wine, lemon juice, oil, and onion juice. Cook, uncovered, 10 to 15 minutes; stir occasionally. Cut pork into 1-inch cubes.

Thread pork, carrots, and pineapple chunks on six skewers; season with salt and pepper. Grill over *medium* coals about 10 minutes; turn frequently. Brush with sauce; grill till done, about 5 minutes more. Makes 6 servings.

KOREAN KABOBS

1½ pounds lean boneless pork
½ cup unsweetened pineapple
    juice
¼ cup soy sauce
¼ cup sliced green onion
    with tops
4 teaspoons sesame seed
1 tablespoon brown sugar
1 clove garlic, minced
⅛ teaspoon pepper
1 teaspoon cornstarch
1 green pepper

Cut pork into 18 pieces. In large bowl combine pineapple juice, soy sauce, green onion, sesame seed, brown sugar, garlic, and pepper; add meat pieces. Cover; refrigerate overnight or let stand 2 hours at room temperature, turning meat occasionally in the marinade.

Drain meat; reserve marinade. In saucepan blend cornstarch and 2 tablespoons water; stir in reserved marinade. Cook and stir till thickened. Cut green pepper into 1-inch squares. Thread pepper on six skewers alternately with meat. Grill over *medium* coals 6 to 8 minutes. Turn kabobs; grill till done, 6 to 8

minutes more, brushing with sauce occasionally. Pass
remaining sauce. Serves 6.

How to
Spit-Roast
a Pig

Obtain a small dressed pig. (Plant on 60 to 70
servings from a 60-pound dressed pig—live
weight, 90 to 100 pounds.)

Rent a large barbecue or follow these general
guidelines for making a barbecue pit. In a grass-
less place, dig a pit 12 inches deep and as wide
and long as the pig. Arrange charcoal in two
lengthwise rows, 12 to 15 inches apart. Drive
notched pipes into ground to hold spit about 16
inches above coals. Rig up motor-driven rotis-
serie. (Or plan to turn spitted pig by hand
throughout roasting period.)

Insert spit rod through center cavity of dressed
pig; test balance. Secure pig well with wires
and/or wire mesh. Tie legs together; cover tail
and ears with foil. Place drip pan between rows
of *hot* coals. Balance spit on pipes. Position drip
pan under pig. Start motor or begin turning.

Pig will shrink as it roasts; have tools handy
to tighten wires. Use a water-filled sprinkler to
put out any flare-ups. (Fires are more frequent
during the first or second hour.) Do not baste
pig. Add *hot* coals to maintain constant heat.

Allow about 8 hours for 60-pound pig to be
done. Time varies with heat of coals and size of
pig. Check doneness by placing meat thermometer in center of thigh of hind leg; make sure it
doesn't touch bone or spit rod. Roast till meat
thermometer registers 170° to 185°. Have large,
clean surface available for carving. Generally,
meat will be so thoroughly cooked that it will fall
off the bones.

ORANGE-GINGER HAM GRILL

¼ cup frozen orange juice
    concentrate, thawed
¼ cup dry white wine
1 teaspoon dry mustard
¼ teaspoon ground ginger
1 1½- to 2-pound fully cooked
    ham slice, cut 1 inch thick
6 canned pineapple slices
  Orange slices (optional)

Combine orange juice concentrate, wine, mustard, and
ginger. Slash fat edge of ham slice. Brush sauce over
ham. Grill over *medium* coals for 10 to 15 minutes,
brushing with sauce occasionally. Turn ham and grill
till done, 10 to 15 minutes more, brushing with sauce.
Grill pineapple slices alongside the ham, brushing frequently with sauce. Place pineapple atop ham during
last 5 to 10 minutes of grilling. Garnish with orange
slices, if desired. Makes 6 servings.

HAM SLICE WITH CRANBERRY SAUCE

1 8-ounce can jellied cranberry
    sauce
2 tablespoons bottled steak
    sauce
1 tablespoon cooking oil
2 teaspoons brown sugar
1 teaspoon prepared mustard
1 1½-pound fully cooked ham
    slice, cut 1 inch thick

Combine jellied cranberry sauce, steak sauce, cooking oil, brown sugar, and prepared mustard. Beat with
electric mixer or rotary beater till smooth.

Slash fat edge of ham slice. Grill over *medium* coals for 10 to 15 minutes, brushing with sauce occasionally. Turn ham and grill till done, 10 to 15 minutes more, brushing with sauce. Heat remaining sauce on edge of grill; serve with ham. Makes 4 or 5 servings.

FRUIT-GLAZED HAM

Apricot Glaze *or*
   Grape Glaze
1 1½-pound fully cooked center
   cut ham slice, cut 1 inch
   thick

Prepare one of the fruit glazes. Slash fat edge of ham slice to prevent curling. Place ham slice in shallow dish; pour glaze mixture over ham. Cover; refrigerate overnight or let stand at room temperature for 2 hours, spooning glaze over ham several times. Remove ham, reserving glaze.

Grill ham slice over *medium* coals for 10 to 15 minutes, brushing with glaze occasionally. Turn ham and grill till done, 10 to 15 minutes more, brushing with glaze. Heat the remaining glaze in small saucepan on edge of grill. To serve cut the ham into slices and pass heated fruit glaze. Makes 6 servings.

Apricot Glaze: In saucepan combine ½ cup apricot preserves, 2 tablespoons prepared mustard, 1 tablespoon water, 2 teaspoons lemon juice, 1 teaspoon Worcestershire sauce, and ⅛ teaspoon ground cinnamon. Heat, stirring occasionally, till preserves melt.

Grape Glaze: In saucepan combine ½ cup grape jelly, 2 tablespoons prepared mustard, 1½ teaspoons lemon juice, and ⅛ teaspoon ground cinnamon. Heat, stirring occasionally, till jelly melts.

ORANGE-SAUCED HAM

1 5-pound boneless fully cooked
   canned ham
1 10-ounce jar currant jelly
¼ cup light corn syrup
2 tablespoons cornstarch
1 teaspoon grated orange peel
⅓ cup orange juice
¾ teaspoon ground nutmeg
   Orange slices
   Parsley sprigs

Insert spit rod through center of ham. Adjust holding
forks; test balance. Insert meat thermometer near
center of ham, not touching rod. In covered grill place
medium coals on both sides of drip pan. Attach spit;
position drip pan under ham. Turn on motor; lower
grill hood or cover with foil tent. Grill ham over
medium coals till done and meat thermometer registers 140°, 1 to 1¼ hours. (If grill does not have spit,
see Note.) Meanwhile, in saucepan combine jelly,
corn syrup, cornstarch, orange peel and juice, and
nutmeg, Cook, stirring constantly, till sauce is thickened. Brush over ham frequently during last 15 minutes of cooking. Heat remaining sauce; pass with ham.
Garnish ham with orange slices and parsley. Serves 12.

Note: If grill does not have spit, place ham directly
on grill over drip pan. Lower hood or tent grill with
heavy-duty foil. Grill ham over *medium* coals for 1
hour. Lift foil tent; turn ham. Insert meat thermometer and brush with sauce. Recover grill with foil tent.
Roast ham till thermometer registers 140°, about 30
minutes more.

SWEET-SOUR HAM

1 5-pound boneless fully cooked
 canned ham
1 20-ounce can pineapple slices
¼ cup dry sherry *or* dry white
 wine
3 tablespoons vinegar
2 tablespoons soy sauce
2 tablespoons honey
1 tablespoon cooking oil
1 clove garlic, minced
 Dash salt
2 small green peppers, cut in
 1½-inch squares
12 cherry tomatoes
2 limes, cut in wedges

Insert spit rod through center of ham. Adjust holding forks; test balance. Insert meat thermometer near center of ham, not touching rod. In covered grill place *medium* coals on both sides of drip pan. Attach spit; position drip pan under meat. Turn on motor; lower grill hood or cover with foil tent. Grill ham over *medium* coals till done and meat thermometer registers 140°, 1 to 1¼ hours. (If grill does not have spit, see Note above.) Meanwhile, drain pineapple, reserving ⅔ cup syrup. Set drained pineapple aside. In saucepan combine the reserved syrup, dry sherry, vinegar, soy, honey, cooking oil, garlic, and salt. Boil mixture down to equal ⅔ cup (about 10 minutes); stir occasionally. During last 30 minutes of cooking, brush ham often with sauce; pass remaining sauce. Before serving, quarter each pineapple slice. Thread 12 small bamboo skewers with green pepper, pieces of pineapple, cherry tomato, and lime wedge. Serve with ham. Serves 12.

SKEWERED HAM AND FRUIT KABOBS

1 8-ounce can pineapple slices
½ cup extra-hot catsup
⅓ cup orange marmalade
2 tablespoons finely chopped onion
1 tablespoon cooking oil
1 to 1½ teaspoons dry mustard
2 pounds fully cooked boneless
     ham, cut into 1-inch cubes
2 oranges, cut in wedges
1 16-ounce jar spiced crab apples

Drain pineapple slices, reserving ⅓ cup syrup. Quarter each pineapple slice and set aside. In saucepan stir together the pineapple syrup, catsup, orange marmalade, onion, oil, and dry mustard. Simmer, uncovered, for about 5 minutes, stirring once or twice.

On six skewers thread ham cubes and orange wedges. Grill over *medium* coals about 15 minutes, turning frequently and brushing with sauce. Thread crab apples and pineapple pieces on ends of skewers. Grill till meat and fruits are hot, 5 to 10 minutes longer, turning the kabobs often and brushing with the sauce. Makes 6 servings.

PINEAPPLE-GLAZED LUNCHEON MEAT

⅔ cup pineapple preserves
⅓ cup packed brown sugar
¼ cup lemon juice
¼ cup prepared mustard
     Whole cloves
3 12-ounce cans luncheon meat

Combine preserves, brown sugar, lemon juice, and mustard. Score each piece of meat in diamonds, cutting only ¼ inch deep. (A strip of heavy paper makes an easy guide for cutting parallel lines.) Stud meat with cloves. Insert spit rod lengthwise through center of each luncheon meat. Secure with holding forks; test balance. In covered grill arrange *hot* coals on both sides of drip pan. Attach spit; position drip pan under meat. Turn on motor; lower grill hood or cover with foil tent. Grill meat over *hot* coals till done, 35 to 40 minutes. During last 10 minutes baste meat often with sauce. Pass remaining sauce. Serves 10 to 12.

MEAT AND POTATO BAKE

4 large baking potatoes
  Cooking oil
1 12-ounce can luncheon meat
4 slices American cheese, cut in
    half diagonally (3 ounces)
  Grated Parmesan cheese
  Butter *or* margarine

Rub potatoes with oil. Wrap each potato in 18×12-inch rectangle of heavy-duty foil; seal edges well. Grill over *medium* coals for 1½ hours; turn frequently. (Or, cook on covered grill over *medium-slow* coals for 1½ to 2 hours.)

Remove from grill; unwrap. Slice each potato crosswise into four pieces. Cut meat in half crosswise; cut each half into six slices crosswise. Insert slices of meat between potato pieces. Reassemble potato; rewrap in foil, closing top. (Or, skewer potato together and omit foil.)

Grill till heated through, 10 to 15 minutes more; turn twice. Remove foil; place 2 cheese triangles atop each potato. Sprinkle with Parmesan; serve with butter. Serves 4.

VEGETABLE-MEAT KABOBS

3 medium yams *or* sweet
    potatoes
1 9-ounce package frozen
    Brussels sprouts
1 12-ounce can luncheon meat
½ cup cooking oil
¼ cup vinegar
½ teaspoon celery seed
1 envelope French salad
    dressing mix
4 to 8 cherry tomatoes

Cook yams, covered, in enough boiling salted water to
cover for 25 to 30 minutes, drain. Cool; peel and cut
into 1-inch chunks. Cook sprouts in boiling salted
water 5 minutes; drain. Cut meat in 1-inch cubes. In
bowl mix oil, vinegar, celery seed, dressing mix, and
dash pepper; blend well. Stir in meat and sprouts.
Cover; refrigerate 4 to 6 hours, stirring often. Drain;
reserve marinade. Thread meat, Brussels sprouts, and
yams on four skewers. Grill over *hot* coals for 5 minutes. Turn; add tomatoes to skewers. Grill till meat is
heated through, about 5 minutes more. Baste often
with reserved marinade. Serves 4.

SUPER-SIMPLE SKILLET SUPPER

1 12-ounce can luncheon meat
1 16-ounce can cut green beans
1½ cups water
1 5½-ounce package dry hash
    brown potatoes with onion
1 5⅓-ounce can evaporated milk
1 5-ounce jar cheese spread
    with hickory smoke flavor

Cut luncheon meat into strips. In skillet combine luncheon meat, undrained green beans, water, dry potatoes, milk, cheese spread, and dash pepper. Cover; cook over *medium* coals, stirring occasionally. Heat till mixture is bubbly and potatoes are tender, about 10 minutes. Serves 4.

Poultry

HICKORY-SMOKED TURKEY

Hickory chips
1 12-pound turkey
1 tablespoon salt
¼ cup cooking oil

Soak hickory chips in enough water to cover, about an hour before cooking. Drain chips. Rinse bird and pat dry; rub cavity with salt. Skewer neck skin to back. Tuck wing tips behind shoulder joints. Push drumsticks under band of skin or tie to tail.

In covered grill arrange *medium-slow* coals around edge of grill. Sprinkle coals with some of dampened chips. Center foil pan on grill, not directly over coals. Place bird, breast side up, in foil pan; brush with oil. Insert meat thermometer in center of inside thigh muscle without touching bone. Lower grill hood. Grill over *medium-slow* coals till thermometer registers 185°, 3½ to 4½ hours. Sprinkle hickory chips over coals every 20 to 30 minutes. Brush bird often with additional oil. Add more coals, if needed. Let the turkey stand 15 minutes before carving. Makes 12 servings.

BARBECUED LEMON TURKEY

1 6- to 7-pound turkey
¼ cup cooking oil
¼ cup soy sauce
¼ cup finely chopped onion
1 teaspoon sugar
1 teaspoon ground turmeric
1 teaspoon ground ginger
½ teaspoon grated lemon peel
2 tablespoons lemon juice

Have meatman cut frozen turkey in half lengthwise. At home thaw turkey. Cut into pieces: 2 wings, 2 drumsticks, 2 thighs, 4 breast pieces, and 2 back pieces.

In large plastic bag combine oil, soy sauce, onion, sugar, turmeric, ginger, lemon peel, and juice. Place turkey pieces in bag; close bag.

Marinate turkey in the refrigerator 6 hours or overnight. Drain, reserving marinade. In covered grill place thighs and breast pieces over *slow* coals. Lower hood and grill about 30 minutes, turning pieces occasionally. Add drumsticks, wings, and back pieces. Lower hood; grill about 1 hour more, turning pieces occasionally. During the last 15 minutes, brush turkey pieces with the reserved marinade. Serves 6 to 8.

SMOKED TURKEY ROAST

Hickory chips
1 3½- to 4-pound frozen
    boneless turkey roast,
    thawed
¼ cup cooking oil
1 tablespoon snipped parsley
2 teaspoons dried sage, crushed
¼ teaspoon lemon pepper
    marinade

Soak the hickory chips in enough water to cover, about an hour before cooking. Drain chips. Insert spit rod through center of turkey roast. Adjust holding forks; test balance. Insert meat thermometer in center of roast, not touching metal rod. In covered grill place *slow* coals on both sides of drip pan. Attach spit; position drip pan directly under roast. Turn on motor. Place a small pan of water at one end of firebox for moisture. Sprinkle coals with some dampened chips; lower grill hood or cover with foil tent. Grill roast over *slow* coals till thermometer registers 185°, 2½ to 3 hours. Brush roast occasionally with mixture of oil, parsley, sage, and lemon pepper. Sprinkle chips over coals every 20 minutes. Let roast stand 10 minutes before carving. Serves 8 to 10.

ROTISSERIE-ROAST TURKEY

6 tablespoons butter *or*
    margarine, melted
¼ cup dry white wine
1 clove garlic, minced
½ teaspoon dried rosemary,
    crushed
1 5- to 6-pound frozen boneless
    turkey roast, thawed
  Salt
  Pepper

Combine *4 tablespoons* of the butter, the wine, garlic, and rosemary. Keep at room temperature to blend flavors.

Insert spit rod through center of turkey roast. Adjust holding forks; test balance. Insert meat thermometer in center of roast, not touching metal rod. Brush roast with remaining 2 tablespoons butter; season with salt and pepper. Place *hot* coals on both sides of foil drip pan. Attach spit; position drip pan directly under roast. Turn on motor. Grill turkey over *hot* coals till thermometer registers 185°, 2½ to 3 hours. During the last

30 minutes, baste roast with wine sauce. Makes 16 to 18 servings.

SWEET-SOUR CORNISH HENS

4 1- to 1½-pound Cornish game
    hens
  Salt
  Pepper
¼ cup butter *or* margarine,
    melted
1 10-ounce jar sweet and sour
    sauce
1 8-ounce can tomatoes, cut up
1 teaspoon soy sauce
6 thin slices lemon, halved

Season cavity of each hen with a little salt and pepper. Skewer neck and tail openings closed. Run spit rod through each hen crosswise, below breastbone. With four 18-inch cords, use one cord to tie each tail to crossed legs. Bring cord around to back, cross and bring around and across breast securing wings to body. Tie knot, cut off loose ends. Space birds about 1 inch apart on rod; secure with holding forks. Test balance. Place *hot* coals on both sides of drip pan. Attach spit; position drip pan under hens. Turn on motor. Grill hens till leg joints move easily, about 45 minutes. Baste hens often with melted butter.

Meanwhile, in saucepan combine sweet and sour sauce, tomatoes, soy sauce, and lemon slices; heat just to boiling. Grill hens about 15 minutes more, basting often with sauce. Pass extra sauce. Makes 4 servings.

CORNISH HENS WITH RICE STUFFING

1 6-ounce package long grain
   and wild rice mix
¼ cup light raisins
2 tablespoons butter *or*
   margarine
2 tablespoons blanched slivered
   almonds
½ teaspoon ground sage
   Salt
4 1- to 1½-pound Cornish game
   hens
¼ cup butter *or* margarine, melted

Cook rice mix according to package directions; stir in raisins, 2 tablespoons butter, almonds, and sage. Rub cavities of each hen with salt. Skewer neck skin to back. Fill each body cavity with about ¾ cup rice stuffing; cover opening with foil. Tie legs to tail; twist wing tips under back. Brush hens with ¼ cup melted butter. Arrange *medium-hot* coals around edge of grill. Center foil pan on grill, not directly over coals. Place birds in foil pan, allowing space between each bird. Grill hens over *medium-hot* coals till tender, 1½ to 1¾ hours. Brush occasionally with the drippings on foil. Serves 4.

KOWLOON DUCKLING

Hickory chips
1 4- to 5-pound duckling
6 to 8 green onions with tops,
  cut up
6 sprigs parsley
1 clove garlic, minced
½ cup soy sauce
2 tablespoons honey
2 tablespoons lemon juice
Plum Sauce

Soak the hickory chips in enough water to cover, about an hour before cooking. Drain chips. Stuff cavity of duckling with onion, parsley, and garlic. Skewer neck and body cavities closed; tie legs to tail securely with cord. In saucepan heat soy sauce, honey, and lemon juice. In covered grill arrange *slow* coals around edge of grill. Sprinkle coals with some of the dampened chips. Center foil pan on grill, not directly over coals. Place duck, breast up, in foil pan. Lower grill hood. Grill for 2¼ to 2½ hours. Sprinkle chips over coals every 30 minutes. Brush duck often with soy mixture. Remove drippings from pan as needed. Serve with Plum Sauce. Serves 2 or 3.

Plum Sauce: Drain one 16-ounce can purple plums, reserving ¼ cup syrup. Force plums through a sieve. In saucepan combine the sieved plums, plum syrup, ¼ teaspoon grated orange peel, 3 tablespoons orange juice, 2 tablespoons sugar, ½ teaspoon Worcestershire sauce, and ¼ teaspoon ground cinnamon. Heat the mixture to boiling; reduce heat and simmer 10 minutes.

GRILLED ISLAND CHICKEN

1 8¼-ounce can crushed
    pineapple
¾ cup packed brown sugar
3 tablespoons lemon juice
1 tablespoon prepared mustard
2 2½- to 3-pound ready-to-cook
    broiler-fryer chickens,
    split in half lengthwise
½ cup cooking oil
1½ teaspoons salt
¼ teaspoon pepper

Drain pineapple and reserve 2 tablespoons syrup.
Combine pineapple, reserved syrup, sugar, lemon
juice, and mustard. Break wing, hip, and drumstick
joints of chickens; twist wing tips under back. Brush
chickens well with oil; season with salt and ¼ teaspoon
pepper. Grill chickens over *slow* coals, bone side down,
till bone side is well browned, 20 to 30 minutes. Turn
chicken; grill till tender, about 30 minutes more. Turn
and brush chickens often with glaze last 10 minutes.
Serves 4.

CORN-STUFFED CHICKEN BREASTS

8 whole chicken breasts
¼ cup chopped onion
¼ cup chopped celery
2 tablespoons butter
1 8¼-ounce can whole kernel
    corn, drained (1 cup)
1 cup herb-seasoned stuffing mix
1 slightly beaten egg
½ teaspoon poultry seasoning
¼ teaspoon salt
¼ cup butter, melted

Cut breasts through white cartilage at V of neck. Using both hands, grasp the small bones on either side. Bend each side back, pushing up with fingers to snap out breastbone, keeping meat in one piece. Do *not* remove skin. Sprinkle cut side with salt. In skillet cook onion and celery in the 2 tablespoons butter till tender. Add corn, stuffing mix, egg, poultry seasoning, and salt; mix well. Spoon some corn mixture on cut side of each chicken breast. Fold over and skewer or tie closed. Grill chicken over *medium-hot* coals till tender, 30 to 35 minutes, turning often. Brush with the ¼ cup melted butter during the last 10 minutes. Serves 8.

CHICKEN TERIYAKI

½ cup packed brown sugar
½ cup soy sauce
2 tablespoons sweet sake, mirin,
    or dry sherry
1 tablespoon grated onion
1 clove garlic, minced
4 whole large chicken breasts,
    split, skinned, and boned
Nonstick vegetable spray
    coating *or* cooking oil

In saucepan stir together brown sugar, soy, sake, onion, and garlic. Cook and stir over low heat till sugar dissolves. Cook, uncovered, till like thin syrup, about 5 minutes more; cool. Place chicken in shallow baking dish. Pour soy mixture over chicken. Cover; refrigerate 4 to 6 hours or overnight, occasionally spooning marinade over.

Remove chicken; reserve marinade. Coat grill with nonstick spray coating or cooking oil. Grill chicken over *medium-hot* coals for 15 to 20 minutes; turn often. Brush frequently with reserved marinade. Serves 8.

SAUSAGE-STUFFED CHICKEN ROLL-UPS

6 whole large chicken breasts,
    skinned and boned
2 tablespoons chopped green
    onion with tops
6 fully cooked smoked sausage
    links
½ cup butter, melted
¼ cup white wine *or* dry sherry
¼ cup snipped parsley
½ teaspoon paprika
    Cooking oil

Place chicken breasts one at a time between two sheets of waxed paper. Working out from center, pound to form 8×8-inch cutlets. Remove paper; sprinkle each cutlet with a little salt and *1 teaspoon* of the green onion. Place a sausage link at the end of each cutlet. Tuck in sides; roll up as for jelly roll. Press end to seal well; secure with wooden picks. Blend next four ingredients. Coat grill with cooking oil. Grill chicken, seam side down, over *medium-hot* coals about 15 minutes, turning often and brushing with butter mixture. Grill till done, 8 to 10 minutes more, turning and brushing with butter mixture. Serves 6.

CHICKEN WITH ZUCCHINI STUFFING

2 2½- to 3-pound whole ready-to-
   cook broiler-fryer chickens
1½ cups chicken broth
⅔ cup regular rice
2 cups chopped zucchini
1 cup shredded carrot
½ cup chopped onion
¾ teaspoon salt
⅛ teaspoon pepper
½ cup chicken broth
¼ cup grated Parmesan cheese
1½ teaspoons dried chervil,
   crushed
   Cooking oil

Sprinkle cavity of birds with salt. In saucepan combine 1½ cups chicken broth and rice. Bring to boiling;
cover. Reduce heat; cook 14 minutes. *Do not drain.* In
another saucepan combine zucchini, carrot, onion, salt,
pepper, and remaining ½ cup broth. Cook, covered, just
till tender, about 10 minutes. *Do not drain.* Stir in
Parmesan cheese and chervil. Fold in rice. Spoon mixture loosely into bird cavities. Skewer neck skin to
back of chickens. Mount one chicken on spit rod (see
tip page 78). Repeat with second fork and chicken.
Add a third holding fork, pressing tines into meat; test
balance. Place *medium* coals around drip pan under
meat. Turn on motor; lower hood or cover with foil
tent. Brush birds with cooking oil. Grill over *medium*
coals till done, about 2 hours. Serves 8.

HERB-GLAZED CHICKENS

2 2½- to 3-pound whole ready-to-
    cook broiler-fryer chickens
½ cup cooking oil
¼ cup light corn syrup
¼ cup finely chopped onion
1 tablespoon lemon juice
1 teaspoon dried oregano,
    crushed
1 teaspoon caraway seed
½ teaspoon salt

Salt chicken cavities. Skewer neck skin to back of
chickens. Mount one chicken on spit rod (see tip page
78). Repeat with second fork and chicken. Add a third
holding fork, pressing tines into meat; test balance.
Place *medium-hot* coals around drip pan. Attach spit;
position drip pan under meat. Turn on motor; lower
hood or cover with foil tent. Grill chickens over *medium-hot* coals till tender, 1½ to 1¾ hours. Position drip
pan under meat. Meanwhile, combine remaining seven
ingredients. Brush over chicken occasionally last 30
minutes. Serves 6 to 8.

How to Mount
Birds for
Spit Roasting

Proper balance and correct timings are the keys to success when spit-roasting. (A) Place one holding fork on spit rod, tines toward point. Insert rod through bird lengthwise. Pinch fork tines together; push into breast. (B) Tie wings, using 24 inches of cord. Start cord at back; loop around each wing. Wrap around wings again. Tie in center of breast. Loop an 18-inch cord around tail, then around crossed legs; tie tightly to hold bird securely. (C) Pull together cords attached to wings and legs; tie tightly. Secure bird with second holding fork.

CURRY BARBECUED CHICKEN

2 2½- to 3-pound ready-to-cook
    broiler-fryer chickens
½ cup cooking oil
1 teaspoon grated lime peel
¼ cup lime juice
1 tablespoon grated onion
1 clove garlic, minced
2 teaspoons curry powder
½ teaspoon salt
½ teaspoon ground cumin
½ teaspoon ground coriander
¼ teaspoon ground cinnamon
¼ teaspoon pepper
    Lime slices
    Parsley

Quarter chickens. Break wing, hip, and drumstick joints of chickens so pieces will remain flat. Twist wing tips under back. Combine cooking oil, lime peel and juice, onion, garlic, curry powder, salt, cumin, coriander, cinnamon, and pepper. Place chickens in large plastic bag set in deep bowl. Pour marinade mixture over chickens. Close bag; refrigerate 4 to 6 hours, turning bag occasionally to coat chickens evenly.

Remove chickens, reserving marinade. Place chicken pieces, bone side down, over *medium-hot* coals. Grill chickens about 25 minutes. Turn, bone side up, and grill till done, 15 to 20 minutes more. Brush chickens with marinade frequently last 10 minutes. Garnish with lime twists and parsley. Makes 8 servings.

CHICKEN AND VEGETABLE BUNDLES

4 chicken drumsticks, skinned
4 chicken thighs, skinned
2 large potatoes, peeled and
   cubed
1 8-ounce can sliced carrots,
   drained
1 8-ounce can cut green beans,
   drained
1 small onion, sliced and
   separated into rings
4 tablespoons butter *or*
   margarine
½ teaspoon dried tarragon,
   crushed
½ teaspoon hickory-smoked salt

Tear off four 18×18-inch pieces of heavy-duty foil. On each piece of foil, place one chicken leg and one thigh; sprinkle chicken with salt and pepper. Top each serving with a *few pieces* of potato, carrots, green beans, and onion. Place 1 tablespoon butter in each bundle; sprinkle each with some of the tarragon and hickory-smoked salt. Bring 4 corners of foil to center, twist securely, allowing room for expansion of steam. Grill the chicken bundles over *slow* coals till chicken is tender, about 1 hour. Makes 4 servings.

SPICY BARBECUED CHICKEN

¼ cup finely chopped onion
1 clove garlic, minced
2 tablespoons cooking oil
¾ cup catsup
⅓ cup vinegar
1 teaspoon grated lemon peel
1 tablespoon lemon juice
1 tablespoon Worcestershire
   sauce
2 teaspoons sugar
1 teaspoon dry mustard
½ teaspoon salt
¼ teaspoon pepper
¼ teaspoon bottled hot pepper
   sauce
2 2½- to 3-pound ready-to-cook
   broiler-fryer chickens

Cook onion and garlic in oil till tender but not brown. Stir in catsup, vinegar, lemon peel and juice, Worcestershire sauce, sugar, dry mustard, salt, pepper, and bottled hot pepper sauce. Simmer, covered, about 30 minutes; stir occasionally. Quarter chickens. Break wing, hip, and drumstick joints of chickens so pieces will remain flat. Twist wing tips under back. Season chicken pieces with additional salt and pepper.

Place chicken pieces, bone side down, over *medium-hot* coals. Grill chickens about 25 minutes. Turn, bone side up, and grill till done, 15 to 20 minutes more. Brush chickens with sauce often last 10 minutes. Makes 8 servings.

LEMONADE CHICKEN

2 2½- to 3-pound ready-to-cook
    broiler-fryer chickens
1 6-ounce can frozen lemonade
    concentrate, thawed
⅓ cup soy sauce
1 teaspoon seasoned salt
½ teaspoon celery salt
⅛ teaspoon garlic powder

Cut the chickens into serving pieces. In small bowl
combine thawed lemonade concentrate, soy sauce,
seasoned salt, celery salt, and garlic powder. Stir mixture to blend well. Dip chicken pieces in lemonade
mixture. Place chicken, bone side down, over *medium-
hot* coals. Grill about 25 minutes. Turn, bone side up,
and grill till done, 15 to 20 minutes more. Brush
chicken with lemonade mixture frequently last 10
minutes. Makes 8 servings.

JAPANESE-STYLE CHICKEN

4 whole large chicken breasts
¼ cup peanut oil *or* cooking
    oil
¼ cup soy sauce
¼ cup dry sherry
1 tablespoon brown sugar
1 tablespoon grated fresh
    gingerroot *or* 1 teaspoon
    ground ginger
1 clove garlic, minced
½ teaspoon salt
18 fresh mushroom caps
3 medium zucchini, cut in 1-inch
    slices (about 18 pieces)

Cut breasts through white cartilage at V of neck. Using both hands, grasp the small bones on either side. Bend each side back, pushing up with fingers to snap out breastbone. To split breast, cut in two lengthwise pieces. Working out from center, pound each to form 5×5-inch cutlet. Cut into strips about 1 inch wide. Combine next seven ingredients. Place chicken in shallow baking dish; pour marinade over. Cover; refrigerate 4 to 6 hours, spooning marinade over occasionally. Remove chicken, reserving marinade. Pour some boiling water over mushrooms in bowl. Let stand 1 minute; drain. On long skewers thread chicken accordion-style alternately with zucchini and mushrooms. Grill over *medium-hot* coals for 12 to 15 minutes; turning and basting often with marinade. Serves 6.

CHICKEN AND BEEF KABOBS

    1 pound beef sirloin steak
    1 14½-ounce can pineapple slices
    ½ cup catsup
    3 tablespoons vinegar
    2 teaspoons instant beef
        bouillon granules
    ¼ cup finely chopped onion
    1 teaspoon celery seed
    ½ teaspoon ground cinnamon
    ¼ teaspoon ground allspice
    1 bay leaf
   12 small whole chicken wings

Cut beef in 1-inch pieces. Drain pineapple; reserve syrup. Cover and refrigerate pineapple. Add water to syrup, if necessary, to measure ¾ cup liquid; combine with catsup, vinegar, bouillon, onion, celery seed, cinnamon, allspice, and bay leaf. Add meat pieces to marinade. Cover; refrigerate several hours, stirring occasionally. Drain meat, reserving marinade. Quarter each pineapple slice; place 2 pieces together. Thread on skewers alternately with beef and chicken. Grill over *hot* coals till done, about 20 minutes, turning and brushing occasionally with reserved marinade. Heat remaining marinade; pass with kabobs. Makes 6 servings.

Microwave Helps to Shorten Grilling Time

Yes, it is possible to get barbecue-flavored chicken in a hurry. The secret: precook chicken pieces in a countertop mirowave oven before putting them on grill. For example, place a single layer of chicken pieces in a 10×6×2-inch baking dish and micro-cook, covered, about 15 minutes. Then grill over *medium-hot* coals till tender, 10 to 15 minutes more; turn chicken till evenly browned.

Fish and Seafood

WINE-SAUCED TROUT

1 15-ounce can tomato sauce
½ cup dry red wine
½ cup butter *or* margarine
2 tablespoons lemon juice
2 tablespoons chopped green
    onion with tops
1 teaspoon sugar
1 teaspoon dried salad herbs
½ teaspoon salt
    Few drops bottled hot pepper
      sauce
6 whole pan-dressed lake *or*
    brook trout *or* perch
    (about 8 ounces each)

In small saucepan combine tomato sauce, wine, butter, lemon juice, green onion, sugar, salad herbs, salt, and hot pepper sauce. Simmer, uncovered, 10 to 15 minutes. Grill fish over *hot* coals 10 to 12 minutes. Turn fish and grill till done, 10 to 12 minutes more. Brush fish with sauce during last few minutes of grilling. Pass the warm sauce. Makes 6 servings.

SKILLET-FRIED FISH

6 fresh *or* frozen pan-dressed
    trout *or* other fish (about 6
    ounces each)
⅔ cup yellow cornmeal
¼ cup all-purpose flour
2 teaspoons salt
1 teaspoon dried parsley flakes
½ teaspoon paprika
1 5⅓-ounce can evaporated
    milk (⅔ cup)
    Cooking oil

Thaw fish, if frozen. Thoroughly stir together cornmeal, flour, salt, dried parsley, and paprika. Dip fish in evaporated milk, then coat with seasoned cornmeal mixture.

Heat a small amount of cooking oil in a large skillet over *hot* coals till oil is hot. Cook fish, a few at a time, in hot oil till lightly browned, 4 to 5 minutes. Turn and cook till fish flakes easily with a fork, 4 to 5 minutes more. Add more oil as needed. Drain the fish on paper toweling before serving. Makes 6 servings.

HICKORY-SMOKED STUFFED TROUT

Hickory chips
¼ cup chopped onion
2 tablespoons butter *or*
      margarine
¼ cup snipped dried apricots
3 tablespoons orange juice
1 teaspoon sugar
1 teaspoon instant chicken
      bouillon granules
¼ teaspoon celery salt
2 cups dry bread cubes
      (2½ slices bread)
2 tablespoons toasted slivered
      almonds
1 4- to 5-pound whole lake
      trout *or* walleyed pike,
      dressed
Cooking oil

About 1 hour before cooking, soak the hickory chips in enough water to cover; drain. In skillet cook onion in butter till tender but not brown. Stir in apricots, orange juice, sugar, bouillon granules, and celery salt. Heat and stir to dissolve bouillon granules. Remove from heat. Add bread cubes and almonds; toss lightly. Spoon stuffing into fish cavity. Brush outside of fish with a little oil.

In covered grill arrange *slow* coals around edge of grill. Sprinkle some of the dampened hickory chips generously over coals. Center foil pan on grill, not directly over coals. Place the fish in foil pan. Close grill hood. Grill till fish flakes easily with fork, about 1¼ hours. Sprinkle hickory chips over the coals every 20 minutes. Makes 8 servings.

BARBECUED FISH

1½ pounds fresh *or* frozen fish
    fillets *or* steaks, *or*
      4 pan-dressed fish (about
      8 ounces each)
½ cup cooking oil
1 tablespoon Worcestershire
    sauce
½ teaspoon onion salt
⅛ teaspoon pepper
    Lemon wedges

Thaw fish, if frozen. Cut fish fillets or steaks into 4 portions. (For pan-dressed fish, wrap tails in greased foil. Sprinkle fish cavities with salt and pepper.) Combine the oil, Worcestershire sauce, onion salt, and pepper; mix well. Place fish in well-greased wire grill basket. Brush fish with oil mixture.

Grill fish over *medium-hot* coals for 5 to 8 minutes. Brush with oil mixture; turn and brush second side. Grill till fish flakes easily when tested with a fork, 5 to 8 minutes more. Serve with lemon wedges. Serves 4.

CRISPY-GRILLED FISH FILLETS

¾ cup finely crushed
    cornflakes
⅛ cup sesame seed, toasted
    (1⅛-ounce container)
1 16-ounce package frozen fish
    fillets, thawed
2 tablespoons soy sauce
    Salt
    Pepper
½ cup dairy sour cream

Combine cornflake crumbs and sesame seed. Brush fish with soy sauce. Season with salt and pepper.

Spread one side of each fillet with sour cream; press coated side in crumb mixture. Repeat spreading with sour cream and coating other side of fillets. Place the coated fish fillets in well-greased wire grill basket. Grill fish over *medium-hot* coals about 8 minutes. Turn fish and grill till fish flakes easily with a fork, about 8 minutes more. Makes 4 servings.

SOY-MARINATED PERCH FILLETS

2 pounds fresh *or* frozen perch
    fillets
⅓ cup cooking oil
3 tablespoons soy sauce
2 tablespoons wine vinegar
2 tablespoons finely chopped
    onion

Thaw fish, if frozen. Place fish fillets in plastic bag set in deep bowl. Combine the cooking oil, soy sauce, wine vinegar, and finely chopped onion; mix well. Pour mixture over fish fillets in bag; close bag. Marinate fish for 30 to 60 minutes at room temperature; turn bag occasionally. Drain fish, reserving marinade.

Place fish in well-greased wire grill basket. Grill over *hot* coals for 8 to 9 minutes. Turn fish and brush with marinade. Grill till fish flakes easily when tested with a fork, 6 to 8 minutes more. Makes 6 servings.

FISH IN A BASKET

⅓ cup all-purpose flour
½ teaspoon salt
⅛ teaspoon pepper
4 whole pan-dressed lake *or*
    brook trout *or* perch (about
    12 ounces each)
¼ cup butter *or* margarine,
    melted

In a bowl combine flour, salt, and pepper. Dip fish in seasoned flour, coating thoroughly. Place the coated fish in a well-greased wire grill basket.

Grill fish over *hot* coals about 10 minutes. Turn fish and baste with melted butter. Grill till fish flakes easily when tested with a fork, about 10 minutes more; baste often with butter. Makes 4 servings.

WILD RICE–STUFFED SALMON

Hickory chips
2 cups chicken broth
¼ cup finely chopped onion
1 cup wild rice, rinsed
1 tablespoon butter *or*
     margarine
1 tablespoon snipped parsley
1 6-pound whole dressed salmon
Butter, melted

Soak the hickory chips in enough water to cover about 1 hour before grilling. Drain chips. In saucepan combine chicken broth and onion; bring to boiling. Add wild rice to saucepan and reduce heat. Cover; simmer till the liquid is absorbed, about 40 minutes. Stir in the 1 tablespoon butter and snipped parsley. Spoon stuffing into cavity of salmon; skewer or tie.

In covered grill arrange *slow* coals around edge of the grill. Sprinkle some of the dampened chips generously over coals. Center foil pan on grill, not directly over coals. Place fish in foil pan.

Close the grill hood. Grill till fish flakes easily when tested with a fork, 1¼ to 1½ hours. Brush fish occasionally with melted butter. Sprinkle the hickory chips over coals every 20 minutes. Makes 10 servings.

STUFFED SMOKED SALMON

Hickory chips
½ cup finely chopped celery
¼ cup chopped onion
3 tablespoons butter *or*
    margarine
4 cups herb-seasoned stuffing
    croutons
2 tablespoons snipped parsley
½ teaspoon grated lemon peel
1 tablespoon lemon juice
½ teaspoon salt
Dash pepper
1 8-pound whole dressed
    salmon
½ cup butter *or* margarine,
    melted

Soak hickory chips in enough water to cover about 1 hour before grilling. Drain chips. In saucepan cook celery and onion in the 3 tablespoons butter till tender. Pour over stuffing croutons. Add parsley, lemon peel and juice, salt, and pepper. Toss together till well combined. Spoon into cavity of salmon; skewer or tie closed.

In covered grill arrange *slow* coals around edge of grill. Sprinkle some of the dampened chips over coals. Center foil pan on grill, not directly over coals. Place fish in foil pan. Close grill hood. Grill till fish flakes easiy when tested with fork, 1¼ to 1½ hours. Brush fish occasionally with melted butter. Sprinkle hickory chips over coals every 20 minutes. Serves 10 to 12.

HALIBUT KABOBS

1 12-ounce package frozen
   halibut steaks, thawed
¼ cup cooking oil
¼ cup dry vermouth
¼ cup lemon juice
1 teaspoon salt
1 teaspoon dried oregano,
   crushed
1 small clove garlic,
   minced
6 mushroom caps
1 large green pepper
12 cherry tomatoes

Cut fish into 1-inch pieces. In bowl combine oil, vermouth, lemon juice, salt, oregano, and garlic. Place fish pieces in marinade. Cover; marinate at room temperature for 1 hour. Drain fish, reserving marinade. Pour some boiling water over mushrooms in bowl. Let stand 1 minute; drain. Cut green pepper into 1-inch squares. On six skewers alternate fish, green pepper, and cherry tomatoes; end with mushroom caps. Grill the kabobs over *medium* coals for 8 to 10 minutes, turning and basting frequently with marinade. Makes 6 servings.

CHARCOALED HALIBUT STEAKS

½ cup shredded unpeeled
    cucumber
½ cup dairy sour cream
¼ cup mayonnaise *or*
    salad dressing
1 tablespoon snipped chives
2 teaspoons lemon juice
¼ teaspoon salt
    Dash pepper
2 pounds fresh *or* frozen halibut
    steaks *or* other fish
¼ cup butter *or* margarine
1 teaspoon salt
⅛ teaspoon pepper
    Paprika

Blend shredded cucumber with sour cream, mayonnaise or salad dressing, chives, lemon juice, the ¼ teaspoon salt, and the dash pepper. Mix well and chill sauce.

Thaw fish, if frozen. Cut into 6 portions. Place in well-greased wire grill basket. In saucepan melt butter; stir in the 1 teaspoon salt and ⅛ teaspoon pepper.

Grill fish over *medium-hot* coals for 5 to 8 minutes, brushing with butter mixture occasionally. Turn and baste with remaining butter mixture. Grill till fish flakes easily when tested with a fork, 5 to 8 minutes more. Sprinkle fish with paprika and serve with chilled cucumber sauce. Makes 6 servings.

CHARCOAL-GRILLED SHRIMP

2 pounds fresh *or* frozen large
    shrimp, shelled and deveined
½ cup olive *or* cooking oil
½ cup finely chopped onion
½ cup dry white wine
¼ cup lemon juice
¼ cup finely snipped parsley
1 tablespoon Worcestershire
    sauce
1 teaspoon dillweed
½ teaspoon salt

Thaw shrimp, if frozen. Combine oil, onion, wine, lemon juice, parsley, Worcestershire, dillweed, and salt. Place shrimp in plastic bag set in deep bowl. Pour marinade mixture over shrimp. Close bag. Marinate 3 to 4 hours in the refrigerator. Drain shrimp, reserving marinade.

Place shrimp in well-greased wire grill basket *or* on 24×18-inch piece of heavy-duty foil. Grill over *hot* coals for 15 to 20 minutes, turning basket or individual shrimp often and basting with marinade. Makes 6 servings.

BARBECUED SHRIMP KABOBS

1 8-ounce can tomato sauce
1 cup chopped onion
½ cup water
¼ cup packed brown sugar
¼ cup cooking oil
¼ cup lemon juice
3 tablespoons Worcestershire
    sauce
2 tablespoons prepared mustard
2 teaspoons salt
¼ teaspoon pepper
1 pound fresh *or* frozen large
    shrimp, shelled and deveined
1 15¼-ounce can pineapple
    chunks
1 green pepper, cut in 1-inch
    squares
2 cups cold water
1 cup regular rice
½ teaspoon salt
2 tablespoons snipped parsley

In saucepan combine tomato sauce, onion, the ½ cup water, brown sugar, cooking oil, lemon juice, Worcestershire, mustard, the 2 teaspoons salt, and pepper. Simmer, uncovered, 15 minutes, stirring once or twice; set aside. Thaw shrimp, if frozen. Drain pineapple, reserving 2 tablespoons syrup. Combine syrup with sauce mixture.

Place shrimp in plastic bag set in a deep bowl. Pour sauce mixture over shrimp; close bag. Marinate at room temperature for 2 to 3 hours. Drain, reserving sauce.

On four skewers alternately thread the shrimp, 2 pineapple chunks, and green pepper squares. Grill over *hot* coals for 5 to 8 minutes. Turn kabobs and brush with marinade. Grill till shrimp are done, 5 to 8 minutes more, basting occasionally with sauce.

Meanwhile, prepare the rice. In a saucepan combine the 2 cups cold water, rice, and ½ teaspoon salt; cover with tight-fitting lid. Bring to a rolling boil; reduce heat. Continue cooking 14 minutes (do not lift cover). Remove from heat; let stand, covered, 10 minutes. Stir in the parsley. Serve hot shrimp kabobs over rice. Pass remaining sauce, if desired. Makes 4 servings.

FOIL-BARBECUED SHRIMP

2 pounds fresh *or* frozen
    large shrimp, shelled
    and deveined
6 tablespoons butter *or*
    margarine
½ cup snipped parsley
¾ teaspoon curry powder
1 clove garlic, minced
½ teaspoon salt
    Dash pepper

Thaw shrimp, if frozen. In saucepan melt butter; stir in parsley, curry powder, garlic, salt, and pepper. Add shrimp; stir to coat. Divide shrimp mixture equally among six 12×18-inch pieces of heavy-duty foil. Fold foil around shrimp, sealing the edges well.

Grill shrimp over *hot* coals about 8 minutes. Turn and grill till done, 7 to 8 minutes more. Serve in foil packages, if desired. Makes 6 servings.

SKEWERED SCALLOPS AND BACON

8 ounces fresh *or* frozen
  unbreaded scallops
  (about 24)
3 tablespoons butter *or*
  margarine, melted
2 tablespoons lemon juice
  Dash pepper
12 bacon slices, halved crosswise
  (12 ounces)
  Paprika

Thaw scallops, if frozen. Remove any shell particles
and wash thoroughly. Combine butter, lemon juice,
and pepper. Pour marinade over scallops. Cover; let
stand at room temperature for 30 minutes. Drain scallops; reserve marinade. In skillet partially cook bacon.
Drain on paper towels and cool. Wrap each scallop
with a half slice of partially cooked bacon. On six
skewers thread bacon-wrapped scallops, securing
bacon with skewer and allowing some space between
each scallop. Sprinkle with paprika. Grill over *hot*
coals, bacon side down, about 5 minutes. Turn, using
spatula; baste with marinade. Grill till bacon is crisp
and brown, about 5 minutes more. Serves 6.

FOIL-WRAPPED CLAMBAKE

48 soft-shelled clams
    in shells
 4 quarts cold water
⅛ cup salt
 2 2- to 2½-pound ready-to-cook
    broiler-fryer chickens,
    quartered
    Salt
    Pepper
 8 whole ears of corn
    Rockweed *or* large bunch
    parsley
 8 frozen lobster tails, thawed
    (about 2 pounds)
 1 16-ounce package frozen fish
    fillets, thawed and cut in
    8 pieces
 1 pound butter, melted

Thoroughly wash clams in shells. In a large kettle combine cold water and ⅛ cup salt. Place clams in salt-water mixture; let stand 15 minutes. Rinse well. Repeat salt-water soaking and rinsing twice more.

Break drumstick, hip, and wing joints of chickens so pieces will remain flat on grill. In covered grill place chicken pieces, skin side down, over *hot* coals. Grill about 10 minutes. Season with salt and pepper. Turn back husks of corn. Use a stiff brush to remove silk. Lay husks back in place.

Tear off sixteen 36x18-inch pieces of heavy-duty foil. Place 1 sheet crosswise over a second sheet. Repeat, making a total of 8 sets. Lay a handful of rockweed or parsley in center of each foil set. Cut eight 18-inch squares of cheesecloth; place 1 square atop rockweed.

For each package arrange the following on cheese-cloth: 6 clams in shells, 1 precooked chicken quarter, 1 ear of corn, 1 lobster tail, and 1 piece of fish. Securely tie opposite ends of cheesecloth together. Seal opposite ends of foil together, sealing edges well.

Place foil packages, seam side up, on grill. Lower the grill hood. Grill over *hot* coals about 45 minutes.

To test for doneness: the chicken drumstick should move up and down easily in socket. Serve with individual cups of hot, melted butter. Makes 8 servings.

GRILLED ROCK LOBSTER TAILS

4 medium frozen rock lobster
    tails
¼ cup butter *or* margarine,
    melted
2 teaspoons lemon juice
1 teaspoon grated orange peel
    Generous dash *each* ground
      ginger, aromatic bitters,
      and chili powder

Thaw rock lobster tails. Cut off thin undershell membrane with kitchen scissors. Bend tail back to crack shell or insert long skewers lengthwise between shell and meat to prevent curling. (To butterfly rock lobster tails, partially thaw tails; snip through center of hard top shell with kitchen scissors. With sharp knife cut through the meat, but *not through undershell*. Spread open.)

Combine melted butter or margarine, lemon juice, orange peel, ginger, aromatic bitters, and chili powder; brush over lobster meat. With meat side up, grill lobster tails over *hot* coals for about 5 minutes. Turn, shell side up, and brush with sauce, grill till meat has lost its transparency and is opaque, 5 to 10 minutes more. Makes 4 servings.

BARBECUED KING CRAB LEGS

¼ cup butter *or* margarine, melted
¼ cup snipped parsley
¼ cup lemon juice
1 tablespoon prepared mustard
2 pounds frozen cooked king crab
    legs, thawed and shelled

Combine butter, parsley, lemon juice, mustard, and ¼ teaspoon salt. Brush the mixture on crab meat. Place crab on grill about 4 inches from *medium* coals. Brush the crab with butter mixture and turn occasionally till heated through, 5 to 8 minutes. Makes 6 servings.

GRILLED SALMON STEAKS

6 fresh *or* frozen salmon steaks
    or other fish steaks
½ cup salad oil
¼ cup snipped parsley
¼ cup lemon juice
2 tablespoons grated onion
½ teaspoon dry mustard
¼ teaspoon salt
    Dash pepper

Thaw fish, if frozen. Place fish in shallow dish. Combine oil, parsley, lemon juice, onion, mustard, salt, and pepper. Pour over fish. Let stand at room temperature 2 hours, turning occasionally. (*Or*, marinate, covered, in refrigerator 4 to 6 hours.) Drain, reserving marinade. Place fish in well-greased wire grill basket. Grill over *medium-hot* coals till fish is lightly browned, 5 to 8 minutes. Baste with marinade and turn. Brush again with marinade; grill till fish flakes easily when tested with a fork, 5 to 8 minutes more. Serves 6.

Basic Cuts of Fish

(A) *Dressed or pan-dressed* fish have been gutted and scaled. Usually, the head, tail, and fins have been removed. (B) *Fillets* are pieces of fish cut lengthwise from the sides of the fish. When filleting a fish, the backbone is discarded intact, so the fillets are virtually boneless. (C) *Steaks* are ⅝- to 1-inch-thick cross-section slices cut from a large dressed fish.

Sausages and Frankfurters

MUSTARD-BRUSHED BOLOGNA KABOBS

1 pound chunk bologna, cut
    into 1-inch cubes
1 15¼-ounce can pineapple
    chunks, drained
¼ cup butter *or* margarine,
    melted
2 tablespoons Dijon-style
    mustard
1 tablespoon snipped parsley
2 teaspoons lemon juice
    Dash pepper

On four skewers alternately thread bologna cubes with pineapple chunks. Combine melted butter, mustard, parsley, lemon juice, and pepper. Brush over skewered bologna and pineapple. Grill kabobs over *medium* coals, turning frequently till heated through, 8 to 10 minutes. Brush the kabobs frequently with the butter mixture. Serves 4.

QUICK FRANK KABOBS

8 frankfurters, cut into
   thirds
1 16-ounce can whole new
   potatoes, drained
2 medium green peppers, cut
   in pieces
¼ cup horseradish mustard
¼ cup catsup
½ envelope taco seasoning mix
   (about 2 tablespoons)
2 tablespoons water
2 tablespoons cooking oil
   Several drops bottled hot
   pepper sauce

Thread frank pieces on skewers alternately with potatoes and pepper pieces. In small bowl stir together horseradish mustard, catsup, taco seasoning mix, water, oil, and hot pepper sauce. Grill kabobs over *medium* coals for 10 minutes, turning often and brushing frequently with mustard mixture. Makes 4 to 6 servings.

TANGY BARBECUED FRANKS

1 medium onion, thinly sliced
¼ cup chopped celery
¼ cup chopped green pepper
1 clove garlic, minced
¼ cup butter *or* margarine
1 10¾-ounce can condensed
    tomato soup
⅓ cup water
¼ cup packed brown sugar
2 tablespoons vinegar
2 tablespoons prepared mustard
1 tablespoon Worcestershire
    sauce
¼ teaspoon bottled hot pepper
    sauce
1 pound frankfurters (8 to 10)

In heavy 10-inch skillet over *hot* coals cook sliced onion, celery, green pepper, and garlic in butter or margarine till tender but not brown, about 10 minutes. Stir in tomato soup, water, brown sugar, vinegar, mustard, Worcestershire, and hot pepper sauce. Cover; bring to boil, allowing 15 to 20 minutes. Score franks on bias; add to hot mixture. Cook till heated through, about 10 minutes more, stirring occasionally. Makes 4 or 5 servings.

JIFFY FRANK AND CABBAGE SKILLET

2 tablespoons butter *or*
    margarine
2 16-ounce jars sweet-sour red
    cabbage, drained
1 12-ounce package frankfurters,
    cut in 1-inch pieces
2 medium apples, cored and
    chopped
1 small onion, chopped

In heavy skillet over *medium* coals melt butter or margarine; stir in drained cabbage, frankfurters, chopped apple, and onion. Cover; simmer mixture till onion is tender and cabbage and meat are heated through, about 20 minutes. Makes 4 servings.

SKEWERED BRATWURST

1 pound bratwurst (6 brats)
¼ cup light cream
2 tablespoons prepared mustard
½ teaspoon instant minced onion
¼ teaspoon coarsely cracked
    pepper
  Dash paprika
1 16-ounce can sauerkraut,
    drained

Cut each brat into thirds. Thread the bratwurst pieces on four skewers. For sauce, combine light cream, mustard, instant minced onion, pepper, and paprika.

Grill brat pieces over *medium-hot* coals till heated through, 7 to 8 minutes; turning and brushing often with sauce. In saucepan heat sauerkraut. Serve grilled meat and sauce over hot sauerkraut. Makes 4 servings.

POLISH SAUSAGE–KRAUTERS

8 slices bacon
8 Polish sausage *or* large
     frankfurters
1 8-ounce can sauerkraut,
     drained and snipped
¼ cup chili sauce
2 tablespoons finely chopped
     onion
1 teaspoon sugar
1 teaspoon caraway seed

Partially cook bacon. Drain; set aside. Slit sausages or frankfurters lengthwise, cutting almost to ends and only ¾ of the way through.

Combine sauerkraut, chili sauce, onion, sugar, and caraway seed. Stuff about 2 tablespoons of the mixture into slit of each sausage or frankfurter. Wrap each with a strip of bacon; secure with wooden picks.

Grill over *hot* coals for 10 to 12 minutes, turning frequently so bacon cooks crisp on all sides. Serves 8.

FRANK AND BEAN SKILLET

1 1¼-ounce envelope sour cream
     sauce mix
¾ cup milk
   Few drops bottled hot pepper
     sauce
1 22-ounce jar baked beans
4 or 5 frankfurters, bias-sliced
1 3-ounce can French-fried
     onions

In heavy skillet blend together sour cream sauce mix, milk, and hot pepper sauce. Stir in baked beans and frank pieces. Cook over *medium* coals, stirring occasionally, till mixture is heated through. Before serving, stir in about ¾ of the French-fried onions. Sprinkle remaining onions atop each serving. Makes 4 servings.

Lamb

MARINATED LEG OF LAMB

1 5- to 6-pound leg of lamb
⅓ cup lemon juice
½ cup cooking oil
¼ cup finely chopped onion
2 tablespoons finely snipped
      parsley
1 teaspoon salt
½ teaspoon dried thyme, crushed
½ teaspoon dried basil, crushed
¼ teaspoon dried tarragon,
      crushed

Have meatman bone leg of lamb and slit lengthwise so you can spread it flat on grill like a thick steak. Combine lemon juice, oil, onion, parsley, salt, thyme, basil, and tarragon. Place lamb in large plastic bag set in deep bowl. Pour lemon juice mixture over lamb; close bag. Refrigerate 4 to 6 hours, turning bag occasionally to coat lamb evenly. Drain lamb, reserving marinade.

Insert two long skewers through meat at right angles making a +, *or* place meat in a wire grill basket. (This makes for easy turning of meat and keeps meat from curling during cooking.) Grill over *medium* coals, turning every 15 minutes, till desired doneness, about 1½ hours for medium or 2 hours for well-done. Baste frequently with reserved marinade. Place lamb on carving board; remove from basket or remove skewers. Cut lamb across grain into thin slices. Makes 8 to 10 servings.

Note: This marinade is equally good on bone-in leg of lamb (see chart on pages 4-5 for timings).

APRICOT LAMB KABOBS

½ cup chopped onion
1 small clove garlic, minced
2 tablespoons cooking oil
1 17-ounce can apricot halves
3 tablespoons vinegar
2 tablespoons brown sugar
½ teaspoon curry powder
Dash bottled hot pepper sauce
1 teaspoon salt
1½ pounds boneless lamb, cut in
1½-inch cubes

In saucepan cook onion and garlic in hot oil till onion is tender but not brown. Place cooked onion, garlic, oil, apricots, vinegar, brown sugar, curry powder, hot pepper sauce, and 1 teaspoon salt in blender container. Cover; blend till smooth. Return mixture to saucepan; simmer, covered, 10 minutes. Cool. Pour mixture over lamb; cover and refrigerate overnight, turning meat occasionally. Drain, reserving marinade. Thread meat on six skewers; grill over *hot* coals for 15 to 20 minutes, turning often. Heat marinade; pass with kabobs. Makes 6 servings.

> ### Balancing
> ### Meat on
> ### a Spit
>
> Meat "done to a turn" on the rotisserie is easy
> once you learn how to balance the meat. To
> mount boneless roasts, insert the spit rod through
> the center of the roast and secure with holding
> forks. Test the balance by holding one end of
> rod in the palm of each hand and turning gently.
> If the meat flops or turns unevenly, readjust
> holding forks or rod as necessary. Bone-in meat
> is harder to balance. To offset the bone's weight,
> insert the rod diagonally. Adjust the holding
> forks and test the balance as above.

SAUCY LAMB RIBLETS

3 to 4 pounds lamb riblets, cut
    in serving-size pieces
½ cup chopped onion
1 tablespoon cooking oil
¾ cup catsup
¼ cup water
3 tablespoons Worcestershire
    sauce
2 tablespoons brown sugar
2 tablespoons vinegar
¾ teaspoon salt
    Dash bottled hot pepper sauce

Trim excess fat from riblets. Cook riblets, covered, in
boiling salted water till tender, 1 to 1¼ hours. Drain.
Meanwhile, cook onion in oil till tender. Add catsup,
water, Worcestershire, brown sugar, vinegar, salt, and
hot pepper sauce; heat through.

Grill riblets over *medium-hot* coals for 10 to 15
minutes; turn. Grill 10 to 15 minutes. Brush riblets
with catsup mixture; continue grilling till riblets are

hot and glazed, 10 to 15 minutes more. Reheat catsup mixture. Brush on riblets before serving; pass with meat. Makes 4 servings.

HERBED LAMB-VEGETABLE KABOBS

½ cup cooking oil
½ cup chopped onion
¼ cup snipped parsley
¼ cup lemon juice
1 teaspoon salt
1 teaspoon dried marjoram,
    crushed
1 teaspoon dried thyme, crushed
1 clove garlic, minced
½ teaspoon pepper
2 pounds boneless lamb, cut in
    1-inch cubes
  Onion wedges
  Green pepper squares
  Sweet red pepper squares

Combine cooking oil, onion, parsley, lemon juice, salt, marjoram, thyme, garlic, and pepper; stir in lamb. Cover; refrigerate 6 to 8 hours, stirring occasionally. Drain lamb, reserving marinade. Cook wedges of onion in water till tender; drain.

Thread six skewers with lamb cubes, onion wedges, green pepper squares, and sweet red pepper squares. Grill over *hot* coals for 10 to 12 minutes; turn and brush often with reserved marinade. Serves 6.

ARMENIAN-ITALIAN LAMB CHOPS

1 cup tomato juice
½ cup finely chopped onion
⅓ cup lemon juice
¼ cup finely chopped dill
    pickle
¼ cup finely chopped
    green pepper
2 tablespoons sugar
1 teaspoon salt
1 teaspoon ground cumin
1 teaspoon dried marjoram,
    crushed
¼ teaspoon pepper
4 teaspoons cornstarch
2 tablespoons cold water
6 lamb shoulder chops, cut
    1 inch thick

In saucepan combine tomato juice, onion, lemon juice, pickle, green pepper, sugar, salt, cumin, marjoram, and ¼ teaspoon pepper. Simmer, covered, till onion and green pepper are tender, about 10 minutes. Blend cornstarch and cold water; stir into sauce. Cook and stir till thickened.

Grill lamb chops over *medium* coals for 10 to 12 minutes. Turn chops and grill till done, 10 to 12 minutes more, brushing frequently with sauce. (Keep sauce warm by placing it in small saucepan on grill.) Pass the remaining sauce with the lamb chops. Makes 6 servings.

BARBECUE SAUCES
AND MARINADES

Want to perk up and improve the smoky flavor of meat cooking on the grill? All you need is a tangy basting sauce or a savory marinade to bring out the flavors of barbecued food. And this chapter features some of the best. Once you have basted a just-right sauce on beef, then next time try it on grilled pork, lamb, poultry, or seafood. Be sure to try the special relishes with different barbecued meats, and savor the flavor combinations.

Sauces and Relishes

SNAPPY BARBECUE SAUCE

1 cup catsup
1 cup water
¼ cup vinegar
1 tablespoon sugar
1 tablespoon Worcestershire
    sauce
1 teaspoon salt
1 teaspoon celery seed
2 or 3 dashes bottled hot
    pepper sauce

In saucepan combine catsup, water, vinegar, sugar, Worcestershire, salt, celery seed, and bottled hot pepper sauce. Bring the mixture to boiling; reduce heat and simmer, uncovered, for 30 minutes. Use to baste pork or beef ribs during last 15 to 20 minutes of barbecuing. Pass remaining sauce. Makes about 2 cups.

EASY BARBECUE SAUCE

1 14-ounce bottle hot-style
   catsup
3 tablespoons vinegar
2 teaspoons celery seed
1 clove garlic, halved

Combine catsup, vinegar, celery seed, and garlic. Refrigerate, covered, for several hours. Remove garlic.
Use to baste hamburgers or beef during last 10 minutes of barbecuing. Makes about 1½ cups sauce.

WESTERN HOT SAUCE

½ cup catsup
¼ cup water
¼ cup finely chopped onion
3 tablespoons red wine vinegar
2 tablespoons cooking oil
2 teaspoons brown sugar
2 teaspoons Worcestershire
   sauce
2 teaspoons whole mustard seed
1 teaspoon paprika
½ teaspoon dried oregano,
   crushed
½ teaspoon chili powder
¼ teaspoon salt
⅛ teaspoon ground cloves
1 bay leaf
1 clove garlic, minced

In saucepan combine catsup, water, onion, vinegar, oil,
brown sugar, Worcestershire, mustard seed, paprika,
oregano, chili powder, salt, cloves, bay leaf, and garlic.
Bring mixture to boiling; reduce heat and simmer,
uncovered, for 10 minutes, stirring once or twice.
Discard bay leaf. Use to baste hamburgers or ribs dur-

ing last 10 to 15 minutes of barbecuing. Makes about
1½ cups.

DURANGO SAUCE

1 16-ounce can pork and beans
    in tomato sauce
1 8-ounce can tomato sauce
½ cup water
1 1¼-ounce envelope chili
    seasoning mix
1 teaspoon Worcestershire sauce

In blender container combine pork and beans in tomato sauce, tomato sauce, water, chili seasoning mix,
and Worcestershire sauce. Cover and blend the mixture till smooth. Use sauce to baste pork chops, steaks,
or hamburgers during last 5 minutes of barbecuing.
Heat remaining sauce to pass. Makes 2½ cups.

MOLASSES-ORANGE BARBECUE SAUCE

1 10¾-ounce can condensed
    tomato soup
1 8-ounce can tomato sauce
½ cup light molasses
½ cup vinegar
½ cup packed brown sugar
¼ cup cooking oil
1 tablespoon instant minced
    onion
1 tablespoon seasoned salt
1 tablespoon dry mustard
1 tablespoon Worcestershire
    sauce
1 tablespoon finely shredded
    orange peeel
1½ teaspoons paprika
½ teaspoon pepper
¼ teaspoon garlic powder

In medium saucepan combine soup, tomato sauce, molasses, vinegar, brown sugar, oil, onion, salt, mustard, Worcestershire, peel, paprika, pepper and garlic powder. Bring to boiling; reduce heat and simmer, uncovered, for 20 minutes. Use to baste poultry or beef during last 15 minutes of barbecuing. Makes about 3½ cups sauce.

CHILI BARBECUE SAUCE

½ cup chili sauce
2 tablespoons cooking oil
2 tablespoons pineapple *or*
    orange juice
1 tablespoon brown sugar
    Dash bottled hot pepper sauce

Combine chili sauce, oil, pineapple or orange juice, brown sugar, and pepper sauce; mix well. Use as a marinade or brush over seafood, chicken, or pork during last 5 to 10 minutes of barbecuing. Makes about ¾ cup.

BIG-BATCH BARBECUE SAUCE

½ cup finely chopped celery
½ cup finely chopped green
    pepper
1 clove garlic, minced
¼ cup butter *or* margarine
4 cups catsup
1 10½-ounce can condensed
    onion soup
1 10½-ounce can condensed
    chicken gumbo soup
2 tablespoons vinegar
½ teaspoon bottled hot
    pepper sauce
½ cup water
1 cup dry white wine

In large saucepan cook celery, green pepper, and garlic in butter or margarine till tender. Stir in catsup, soups, vinegar, hot pepper sauce, and ½ cup water. Simmer mixture 30 minutes, stirring occasionally. Stir in wine. Pour into 1- or 2-cup freezer containers. Seal, label, and freeze. To use, thaw the sauce. Use to baste chicken, frankfurters, ribs, or steaks the last 10 to 15 minutes of barbecuing. Heat the remaining sauce to pass, if desired. Makes 8 cups sauce.

PINEAPPLE-ORANGE GLAZE

½ of a 6-ounce can frozen
    pineapple juice concentrate
¼ cup orange marmalade
2 tablespoons bottled
    steak sauce

In saucepan combine pineapple concentrate, marmalade, and steak sauce. Cook and stir the mixture till heated through. Use to baste poultry or pork during the last 10 to 15 minutes of barbecuing. Makes about ⅔ cup.

TARRAGON-CIDER BASTING SAUCE

½ cup apple cider *or* juice
¼ cup vinegar
¼ cup sliced green onion
    with tops
2 tablespoons butter *or*
    margarine
2 tablespoons bottled steak
    sauce
2 tablespoons honey
1 teaspoon salt
1 teaspoon dried tarragon,
    crushed
¼ teaspoon pepper

In a 1½-quart saucepan combine cider, vinegar, onion, butter, steak sauce, honey, salt, tarragon, and pepper. Bring to boiling; simmer, uncovered, for 20 minutes, stirring mixture occasionally. Use as a meat marinade or use to baste chicken, beef, pork, or fish during last 15 to 20 minutes of barbecuing. Heat and pass the remaining sauce. Makes about ¾ cup sauce.

COFFEE-SOY GLAZE

½ cup packed brown sugar
1 tablespoon cornstarch
⅔ cup cold strong coffee
¼ cup soy sauce
3 tablespoons wine vinegar

In a small saucepan blend together the brown sugar and cornstarch. Add coffee, soy sauce, and vinegar; mix well. Cook and stir mixture till thickened and bubbly. Use to baste spareribs or pork chops during the last 15 minutes of barbecuing. Makes about 1 cup sauce.

SOY-LEMON BASTING SAUCE

1 tablespoon brown sugar
1 teaspoon cornstarch
2 tablespoons lemon juice
2 tablespoons soy sauce
2 tablespoons water
2 tablespoons sliced green
    onion with tops
1 tablespoon butter *or* margarine
1 clove garlic, minced

In saucepan blend brown sugar and cornstarch. Stir in lemon juice, soy sauce, and water. Add onion, butter, and garlic. Cook and stir till thickened and bubbly.

Use to baste poultry or fish during last 15 minutes of barbecuing. Makes about ⅓ cup.

SEASONED BUTTER LOG

¼ cup butter, softened
2 tablespoons braunschweiger
2 teaspoons lemon juice
¼ teaspoon dried basil, crushed
Paprika

Blend together softened butter, braunschweiger, lemon juice, and basil. Shape into a 4-inch log on waxed paper. Roll log in paprika to coat. Chill till firm. Slice butter log and serve with grilled steaks.

CARAWAY-CHEESE SPREAD

1 3-ounce package cream
cheese, softened
1 tablespoon butter, softened
1 teaspoon caraway seed
1 teaspoon prepared mustard

In a small bowl blend together cream cheese and softened butter. Stir in caraway seed and mustard. Spread atop grilled hamburgers. Makes about ½ cup.

ZESTY SAUERKRAUT RELISH

½ cup sugar
½ cup vinegar
1 teaspoon prepared mustard
¼ teaspoon garlic powder
¼ teaspoon pepper
1 16-ounce can sauerkraut,
    drained
⅓ cup chopped sweet red *or*
    green pepper
⅓ cup chopped onion
⅓ cup chopped cucumber

In saucepan heat sugar and vinegar till sugar is dissolved; stir occasionally. Stir in mustard, garlic powder, and pepper. Cool. Combine drained sauerkraut, red or green pepper, onion, and cucumber; stir together with the vinegar mixture. Cover and chill the relish till needed. Makes about 3 cups relish.

CUCUMBER RELISH

3 large tomatoes, chopped
1 medium cucumber, peeled,
    seeded, and chopped (1 cup)
¼ cup chopped fresh coriander
    leaves
3 tablespoons finely chopped
    onion
¼ teaspoon finely chopped
    canned green chili peppers
1 tablespoon lemon juice
½ teaspoon salt

Combine tomatoes, cucumber, coriander leaves, onion, and chili peppers. Stir together lemon juice and salt. Add to the vegetable mixture and mix well. Cover and chill till needed. Makes about 2⅔ cups relish.

SANDWICH COLESLAW

2 cups finely shredded cabbage
⅓ cup thinly sliced green onion
   with tops
¼ cup snipped parsley
2 tablespoons sugar
3 tablespoons vinegar
1 teaspoon salt
½ teaspoon celery seed
   Dash bottled hot pepper sauce

Combine the shredded cabbage, green onion, and parsley. Stir together sugar, vinegar, salt, celery seed, and hot pepper sauce. Pour over cabbage mixture and toss. Cover and chill till needed. Makes about 2 cups relish.

RATATOUILLE RELISH

2 medium green peppers, stems
   and seeds removed
2 tomatoes, cored
1 medium onion
1 medium zucchini
½ of a small eggplant, peeled
2 tablespoons salt
1 cup sugar
1 cup vinegar
1 cup water
1 teaspoon whole mustard seed
¾ teaspoon celery seed
¼ teaspoon fines herbs

Using coarse blade of food chopper, grind peppers, tomatoes, onion, zucchini, and eggplant. Stir salt into vegetables. Cover; refrigerate and let stand overnight. Rinse and drain vegetables. In saucepan combine

sugar, vinegar, water, mustard seed, celery seed, and
fines herbs. Stir in vegetables. Bring mixture to boiling;
reduce heat and simmer 5 minutes, stirring frequently.
Cool. Cover and chill till needed. Makes about 4 cups
relish.

RED PEPPER RELISH

6 sweet red peppers
   (about 1½ pounds)
2 medium onions, quartered
¾ cup sugar
¾ cup vinegar
1½ teaspoons salt

Remove stems and seeds from red peppers. Using
coarse blade of food chopper, grind peppers and
onions, reserving juices. In Dutch oven or large saucepan combine peppers and onions and reserved juices.
Stir in sugar, vinegar, and salt. Bring to boiling; boil
gently, uncovered, for 20 to 25 minutes. Cool; cover
and chill till needed. Makes about 2 cups relish.

Marinades

ARMENIAN HERB MARINADE

½ cup olive oil *or* cooking oil
½ cup chopped onion
½ cup tomato juice
¼ cup lemon juice
¼ cup snipped parsley
1 teaspoon salt
1 teaspoon dried marjoram,
   crushed
1 teaspoon dried thyme, crushed
½ teaspoon pepper
1 clove garlic, minced

Combine oil, chopped onion, tomato juice, lemon juice, parsley, salt, marjoram, thyme, pepper, and garlic. Place lamb, pork, or chicken in a plastic bag set in a deep bowl or a shallow baking dish. Pour marinade mixture over meat. Close bag or cover dish; refrigerate 4 to 6 hours or overnight. Turn the bag or spoon marinade over the meat occasionally to coat evenly. Makes 1¾ cups (enough for 3 to 4 pounds meat).

SAVORY WINE MARINADE

1 small onion
½ cup cooking oil
½ cup white wine
¼ cup lime juice *or* lemon juice
2 tablespoons snipped parsley
½ teaspoon salt
¼ teaspoon bottled hot
    pepper sauce

Thinly slice the onion; separate into rings. Combine oil, wine, lime juice, parsley, salt, and pepper sauce; add onion. Place fish or chicken in a plastic bag set in a deep bowl or a shallow baking dish. Pour marinade mixture over meat. Close bag or cover dish; refrigerate for 4 to 6 hours or overnight. Turn the bag or spoon marinade over the meat occasionally to coat evenly. Makes about 1½ cups (enough for 3 pounds meat).

TERIYAKI MARINADE

¼ cup cooking oil
¼ cup soy sauce
¼ cup dry sherry
1 tablespoon grated fresh
    gingerroot *or* 1 teaspoon
    ground ginger
1 clove garlic, minced
2 tablespoons molasses

Combine oil, soy sauce, dry sherry, ginger, and garlic. Place chicken, beef, or pork in plastic bag set in deep bowl or a shallow baking dish. Pour marinade mixture over meat. Close bag or cover dish; refrigerate 4 to 6 hours or overnight. Turn bag or spoon marinade over meat occasionally to coat evenly. Drain, reserving marinade. Stir in molasses. Use to baste meat during last 10 minutes of barbecuing. Makes about 1 cup (enough for 2 pounds meat).

HERB-SEASONED MARINADE

¼ cup cooking oil
¼ cup wine vinegar
¼ cup finely chopped onion
1 tablespoon Worcestershire
  sauce
½ teaspoon dried basil, crushed
½ teaspoon dried rosemary,
  crushed
¼ teaspoon pepper
⅛ teaspoon bottled hot
  pepper sauce
½ teaspoon salt

Combine oil, vinegar, onion, Worcestershire, basil, rosemary, pepper, hot pepper sauce, and ½ teaspoon salt. Place beef, pork, or chicken in a plastic bag set in a deep bowl or a shallow baking dish. Pour marinade mixture over meat. Close bag or cover dish; refrigerate 4 to 6 hours or overnight. Turn bag or spoon marinade over meat occasionally to coat evenly. Makes about ¾ cup (enough for 2 pounds meat).

GRILL-SIDE RECIPES

Meat grilled to flavor perfection is only the beginning of an outstanding backyard menu. It's the tantalizing accompaniments that really make a good meal great. Each of the recipes in this chapter, whether it's an appetizer hot off the grill or one of the many vegetables, breads, or desserts, will keep your family and friends coming back for more. All of these recipes cook right on the grill along with the meat while it barbecues.

Vegetables

SWEET HERBED TOMATOES

6 medium tomatoes, peeled
2 medium cucumbers, scored and
    thinly sliced (3½ cups)
½ cup salad oil
¼ cup dry white wine
¼ cup white wine vinegar
2 tablespoons snipped chives
1 tablespoon snipped parsley
1 tablespoon sugar
1 tablespoon dried salad herbs,
    crushed
⅛ teaspoon freshly ground pepper
1 teaspoon salt

Lightly sprinkle tomatoes with salt. In large deep bowl place whole tomatoes and sliced cucumbers. In screw-top jar combine salad oil, dry white wine, white wine vinegar, chives, parsley, sugar, salad herbs, pepper, and 1 teaspoon salt; cover and shake vigorously. Pour over vegetables. Cover and chill several hours or overnight to thoroughly blend flavors. Turn tomatoes once or twice.

Remove tomatoes, reserving cucumbers in marinade. Wrap *each* tomato in a 6-inch square of heavy-duty foil. Grill over *medium* coals till heated through, about 20 minutes, turning once. Drain cucumbers; reserve marinade to store leftovers. Serve cucumbers atop tomatoes. Serves. 6.

GRILLED ACORN SQUASH

3 medium acorn squash
2 tablespoons butter *or*
    margarine
2 tablespoons brown sugar
2 tablespoons water
    Brown sugar
1 apple, cut into wedges

Rinse squash. Cut in half lengthwise; remove seeds. Prick inside with tines of fork; season cavities with salt and pepper. Add *1 teaspoon* each of butter, brown sugar, and water to each squash. Wrap each half, cut side up, in 12x18-inch piece of heavy-duty foil; seal securely. Place cut side up on grill. Grill over *medium* coals till tender, 50 to 60 minutes. Open; stir to fluff squash; sprinkle with additional brown sugar. Top with wedges. Serves 6.

CHEESY POTATO-CARROT FOIL BAKE

4 slices bacon
3 large potatoes
3 medium carrots, shredded
¼ cup sliced green onion with
    tops
  Salt
  Pepper
¼ cup butter *or* margarine
½ teaspon caraway seed
1 cup shredded Monterey Jack
    cheese (4 ounces)

Cook bacon till crisp; drain and crumble. Set aside. Tear off a 36x18-inch piece of heavy-duty foil. Fold in half to make an 18-inch square. Fold up sides, using fist to form a pouch. Thinly slice potatoes into pouch; add carrots and green onion. Sprinkle with salt and pepper; dot with butter and sprinkle with caraway. Fold edges of foil to seal pouch securely, leaving space for expansion of stream. Grill over *slow* coals till done, 55 to 60 minutes; turn several itmes. Open package; stir in crumbled bacon and cheese. Close pouch; return to grill till cheese melts, about 1 minute. Serves 6.

VEGETABLES ON A STICK

6 small onions
5 small pattypan squash
2 sweet red peppers
¼ cup butter *or* margarine
¼ teaspoon salt
  Dash pepper

Cook onions in small amount of boiling salted water till nearly tender, about 25 minutes; drain. Quarter squash; cut red peppers into large squares. In small saucepan heat butter with salt and pepper till butter melts.

On four skewers alternately thread vegetables. Grill over *medium* coals till done, 20 to 25 minutes; turning and brushing often with butter sauce. Serves 4.

HERBED ONION SLICES

3 tablespoons butter
1 tablespoon brown sugar
½ teaspoon salt
2 large onions, cut into
    ½-inch slices
¼ cup finely chopped celery
2 tablespoons finely snipped
    parsley
2 tablespoons grated Parmesan
    cheese
¼ teaspoon dried oregano,
    crushed

In large heavy skillet melt butter over *medium-slow* coals; stir in brown sugar, ½ teaspoon salt, and dash pepper. Place onion slices in a single layer in butter mixture. Sprinkle celery over all. Cover; cook slowly for 10 minutes. Turn onion slices; sprinkle with parsley, Parmesan, and oregano. Cook, covered, 10 minutes more. Serves 4.

HERBED-SEASONED VEGETABLES

8 small onions
4 large carrots, cut in 1½-inch
     pieces
4 small pattypan squash
2 green peppers
¼ cup butters, melted
¼ teaspoon dried rosemary,
     crushed
¼ teaspoon dried marjoram,
     crushed
¼ teaspoon salt

In saucepan cook onions and carrots in small amount of boiling salted water till nearly tender, about 20 minutes; drain. Cut squash into 1-inch wedges; cut peppers into 1-inch squares. Combine butter, rosemary, marjoram, ¼ teaspoon salt, and dash pepper.

On four skewers alternately thread vegetables. Grill over *medium* coals till done, about 20 minutes; turn and brush frequently with butter mixture. Serves 4.

CORN WITH CHIVE SAUCE

6 ears corn
½ cup chopped celery
1 2-ounce jar sliced pimiento,
     chopped
1 4-ounce container whipped
     cream cheese with chives
2 tablespoons milk
¼ teaspoon salt
   Dash pepper

Using a sharp knife, cut off tips of corn kernels; carefully scrape cobs with dull edge of knife. Combine corn, celery, pimiento, cheese, milk, salt, and pepper; mix well.

Tear off a 36x18-inch piece of heavy-duty foil. Fold in half to make an 18-inch square; fold up sides slightly. Spoon corn mixture onto center of foil. Fold edges of foil to seal securely, leaving space for expansion of steam. Grill over *medium-hot* coals till tender, about 40 minutes; turn occasionally. Serves 6.

EGGPLANT-TOMATO STACK-UPS

12 slices eggplant, cut ½ inch
    thick
    Seasoned salt
3 to 4 tablespoons butter *or*
    margarine
6 thick slices tomato
6 slices process Swiss cheese,
    halved

Sprinkle eggplant with seasoned salt. In skillet fry eggplant on range top on both sides in butter till nearly tender, about 5 minutes. Tear off six 6-inch squares of heavy-duty foil; place *one* eggplant slice on *each* piece of foil. Top each with *one* tomato slice and a *half slice* cheese; cover with remaining eggplant slices, then remaining cheese. Seal foil packets loosely. Grill over *medium* coals till heated through, 5 to 8 minutes. Serves 6.

CHEESE-TOPPED TOMATOES

2 tomatoes
¾ cup soft bread crumbs
½ cup shredded sharp American
    cheese (2 ounces)
2 tablespoons butter, melted
2 tablespoons snipped parsley

Slice each tomato in half crosswise. Sprinkle cut surfaces with a little salt and pepper. Combine bread crumbs, cheese, and butter; sprinkle over tomatoes. Garnish with parsley. Wrap each tomato half loosely in a 6-inch square of heavy-duty foil. Grill over *medium-hot* coals till heated through, 15 to 20 minutes. Makes 4 servings.

CHEESE-SAUCED PEAS AND MUSHROOMS

1 10-ounce package frozen peas
    with sliced mushrooms
½ cup light cream
¼ cup shredded process Swiss
    cheese *or* American cheese
2 tablespoons snipped chives
1 clove garlic, minced

Tear off a 36x18-inch piece of heavy-duty foil. Fold in half to make an 18-inch square. Fold up sides, using fist to make a pouch. Place frozen peas with sliced mushrooms in pouch. Add light cream, cheese, chives, garlic, dash salt, and dash pepper. Fold edges of foil to seal pouch securely, leaving space for expansion of steam. Grill over *medium-hot* coals till heated through, about 20 minutes. Transfer to serving bowl. Makes 4 servings.

BROCCOLI IN FOIL

2 10-ounce packages frozen
    broccoli spears
  Seasoned salt
  Pepper
3 tablespoons water
2 tablespoons butter *or*
    margarine
  Lemon slices

Tear off a 36x18-inch piece of heavy-duty foil. Fold in half to make an 18-inch square. Fold up sides, using fist to form pouch. Place frozen broccoli in center of pouch. Sprinkle with seasoned salt and pepper. Add water; dot with butter. Fold edges of foil to seal securely, leaving space for expansion of steam. Grill over *medium-slow* coals till done, about 60 minutes, turn often. Garnish with lemon slices. Makes 6 servings.

YELLOW LEMON RICE

1⅓ cups quick-cooking rice
1⅓ cups water
 2 tablespoons lemon juice
 2 teaspoons ground turmeric
 1 teaspoon mustard seed
 ¾ teaspoon salt
 2 tablespoons butter *or*
      margarine

Tear off a 36x18-inch piece of heavy-duty foil. Fold in half to make an 18-inch square. Fold up sides, using fist to form a pouch. In bowl thoroughly combine rice, water, lemon juice, ground turmeric, mustard seed, and salt. Place mixture in pouch; dot with butter. Fold edges of foil to seal pouch securely. Grill over *medium-hot* coals till done, 15 to 20 minutes. Before serving, open pouch and fluff rice with a fork. Makes 4 servings.

ZUCCHINI FRITTERS

⅓ cup packaged biscuit mix
¼ cup grated Parmesan cheese
⅛ teaspoon pepper
 2 slightly beaten eggs
 2 cups shredded unpeeled
      zucchini (2 medium)
 2 tablespoons butter

In bowl stir together biscuit mix, Parmesan cheese, and pepper. Stir in beaten eggs just till mixture is moistened. Fold in zucchini. In large heavy skillet or griddle melt butter over *medium-hot* coals. Using 2 tablespoons mixture for each fritter, cook four at a time till browned, 4 to 5 minutes on each side. Keep warm while cooking remaining zucchini fritters. Makes 6 servings.

MARINATED VEGETABLE KABOBS

1 10-ounce package frozen
    Brussel sprouts
⅓ cup salad oil
¼ cup vinegar
1 clove garlic, minced
1 teaspoon celery seed
1 teaspoon dried parsley flakes,
    crushed
½ teaspoon salt
¼ teaspoon dried basil, crushed
¼ teaspoon pepper
4 tomatoes, cut in wedges
4 ounces fresh mushrooms
2 small cucumbers, cut in 1-inch
    slices

Cook Brussels sprouts in boiling salted water till barely tender, about 5 minutes; drain. Meanwhile, in screw-top jar combine salad oil, vinegar, garlic, celery seed, parsley flakes, salt, basil, and pepper; cover and shake well. Place Brussels sprouts, tomatoes, mushrooms, and cucumbers in plastic bag set in deep bowl. Pour marinade mixture over vegetables. Close bag; refrigerate 6 to 8 hours or overnight, stirring occasionally. Drain vegetables, reserving marinade. On six skewers thread Brussels sprouts, tomatoes, mushrooms, and cucumbers. Grill over *medium* coals till heated through, 15 to 20 minutes, turning and brushing frequently with marinade mixture. Serves 6.

ROASTED CORN ON THE COB

½ cup butter *or* margarine,
    softened
1 teaspoon salt
½ teaspoon dried rosemary,
    crushed
½ teaspoon dried marjoram,
    crushed
6 ears corn

Cream together butter and salt till fluffy. Combine herbs and blend into butter. Keep mixture at room temperature for 1 hour to blend flavors. Turn back husks of corn; remove silks with stiff brush. Place each ear on a piece of heavy-duty foil. Spread corn with about *1 tablespoon* of the butter. Lay husks back in position. Wrap corn securely. Roast ears directly on *hot* coals; turn frequently till corn is tender, 12 to 15 minutes. Or, on covered grill with an elevated rack, roast corn according to manufacturer's directions. Serves 6.

ANISE CORN

1 12-ounce can whole kernel corn,
    drained
2 tablespoons butter *or*
    margarine
¼ teaspoon anise seed, crushed
    Dash salt
    Dash pepper

Tear off a 36x18-inch piece of heavy-duty foil. Fold in half to make an 18-inch square. Fold up sides, using fist to make a pouch. Place corn in pouch; dot with butter. Sprinkle anise seed over all; add salt and pepper. Fold edges of foil to seal pouch securely, leaving space for expansion of steam. Grill over *medium-hot* coals till heated through, 15 to 20 minutes. Makes 4 servings.

Frozen Vegetables Hot off the Grill

Utilize your grill to best advantage by cooking frozen vegetables alongside the meat. It's easy. Here's how: Tear off a 36x18-inch piece of heavy-duty foil. Fold in half to make an 18-inch square. Fold up sides, using fist to form pouch. Place one 10-ounce package of frozen vegetables in center of pouch. Season with salt and pepper; top with a pat of butter or margarine. Fold edges of foil to seal pouch securely, leaving space for expansion of steam. Grill over *medium-hot* coals till vegetables are cooked (allow about 20 minutes for peas and other small vegetables; allow longer for larger vegetables). Turn package frequently.

CHEESY EGGPLANT SLICES

1 medium eggplant, peeled and
    sliced ¾ inch thick
    (about 1 pound)
¼ cup butter *or* margarine,
    melted
⅓ cup finely crushed round cheese
    crackers (16 crackers)
4 slices mozzarella *or* Swiss
    cheese, cut in half diagonally

Tear off four 18x18-inch pieces of heavy-duty foil. Sprinkle eggplant slices with salt and pepper. Dip each eggplant slice into melted butter, then into crushed cheese crackers. Place *two* slices of eggplant on *each* square of foil. Wrap foil loosely around egg-plant, sealing edges securely. Grill packets over *medium* coals about 10 minutes. Turn and grill till eggplant is done, 6 to 7 minutes more. Open foil and top *each* eggplant slice with *one* cheese triangle. Makes 4 servings.

WHOLE GRILLED POTATOES

6 potatoes
  Cooking oil
  Shredded Swiss cheese
  Sliced green onion with tops

Tear off six 6x6-inch pieces of heavy-duty foil. Brush potatoes with some cooking oil. Wrap *one* potato in *each* 6-inch square of foil. Place on covered grill; lower the hood. Grill over *medium-slow* coals till tender, 1½ to 2 hours, turning occasionally. Open potatoes with tines of fork and push ends to fluff. Top with shredded cheese and sliced green onion. Makes 6 servings.

BARBECUED-STYLE SPANISH RICE

1 16-ounce can tomatoes, cut up
1 cup quick-cooking rice
½ cup finely chopped green
   pepper
¼ cup finely chopped onion
¼ cup water
2 teaspoons Worcestershire
   sauce
1 teaspoon sugar
¾ teaspoon salt
½ teaspoon chili powder
½ teaspoon dried basil, crushed
1 tablespoon butter *or* margarine

In heavy 8-inch skillet combine undrained tomatoes, rice, green pepper, onion, water, Worcestershire sauce, sugar, salt, chili powder, and basil; dot mixture with butter. Cover skillet and cook over *medium-hot* coals till done, 20 to 25 minutes, stirring occasionally. Before serving, fluff rice with fork. Makes 4 servings.

CALICO RICE BAKE

  1 16-ounce can mixed vegetables,
      drained
  1⅓ cups quick-cooking rice
  1⅓ cups water
  1 cup shredded sharp Cheddar
      cheese (4 ounces)
  ¾ teaspoon salt
  ½ teaspoon onion salt
  ¼ teaspoon dried rosemary,
      crushed
  ⅛ teaspoon pepper
  2 tablespoons butter *or*
      margarine

Tear off a 36x18-inch piece of heavy-duty foil. Fold in half to make a 18-inch square. Fold up sides, using fist to form a pouch. In bowl thoroughly combine vegetables, rice, water, cheese, salt, onion salt, rosemary, and pepper. Place mixture in pouch; dot with butter. Fold edges of foil to seal pouch securely. Grill over *medium-hot* coals till done, about 30 minutes. Before serving, open pouch and fluff rice with a fork. Serves 6.

SKILLET FRENCH FRIES

3 tablespoons butter *or*
      margarine
½ envelope onion soup mix
1 16-ounce package frozen
      French-fried crinkle-cut
      potatoes
½ cup shredded sharp American
      cheese (2 ounces)

In heavy skillet melt butter over *medium-hot* coals;
stir in dry onion soup mix. Add frozen potatoes; stir
to coat evenly. Heat potatoes over *medium-hot* coals,
turning as needed with wide spatula, till browned and
heated through, 15 to 20 minutes. Remove from heat.
Top with cheese; toss lightly and serve at once. Makes
6 servings.

ITALIAN-SEASONED VEGETABLE KABOBS

   Boiling water
12 fresh large mushrooms
 2 small zucchini, cut in 1-inch
      bias-sliced pieces
 3 tablespoons Italian salad
      dressing
 2 tablespoons lemon juice
 1 teaspoon Worcestershire
      sauce
¼ teaspoon salt
12 cherry tomatoes

Pour some boiling water over mushrooms in a bowl.
Let stand 1 minute; drain. On four skewers alternately
thread mushrooms and zucchini. Combine Italian salad
dressing, lemon juice, Worcestershire sauce, and salt.
Grill kabobs over *medium* coals about 12 minutes,

turning and brushing often with salad dressing mixture. Thread cherry tomatoes on ends of skewers; grill till heated through, 5 to 8 minutes more, turning and brushing often with salad dressing mixture. Makes 4 servings.

CURRY BUTTERED POTATOES

3 tablespoons butter *or*
    margarine
1 teaspoon curry powder
6 medium potatoes, peeled and
    thinly sliced
¾ teaspoon salt
⅛ teaspoon pepper
1 cup chopped onion
¼ cup finely snipped parsley

In heavy skillet melt butter over *medium* coals; stir in curry powder. Sprinkle potatoes with salt and pepper. Add sliced potatoes and onion. Cover skillet and cook over *medium* coals about 20 minutes. Thoroughly stir mixture and sprinkle parsley atop. Cook potatoes till browned and tender, about 20 minutes more. Makes 6 servings.

HOT-STYLE BEANS AND TOMATOES

8 ounces fresh green beans,
    cut in 1-inch pieces
2 tomatoes, sliced
¼ cup chopped onion
¼ cup butter *or* margarine,
    softened
1 tablespoon brown sugar
2 teaspoons prepared mustard
1 teaspoon salt
1 teaspoon prepared horseradish

In saucepan cook green beans in a little boiling water for 10 minutes; drain. Tear off a 36x18-inch piece of heavy-duty foil. Fold in half to make an 18-inch square. Fold up sides, using fist to form pouch. Place drained green beans and tomato slices in center of pouch. Combine chopped onion, butter, brown sugar, mustard, salt, horseradish, and dash pepper; beat till fluffy. Dot butter mixture over beans and tomatoes. Fold edges of foil to seal pouch securely, leaving space for expansion of steam. Grill over *medium-hot* coals till heated through, 30 to 35 minutes. Makes 4 or 5 servings.

HERBED GREEN BEANS

1 16-ounce can French-style
    green beans, drained
⅓ cup chopped celery
¼ cup chopped sweet red *or* green
    pepper
1 bay leaf
¼ teaspoon dillweed
2 tablespoons butter *or*
    margarine

Combine beans, celery, red or green pepper, bay leaf, dillweed, and dash salt. Tear off an 18-inch square of heavy-duty foil. Place bean mixture in center of foil; top with butter or margarine.

    Fold edges of foil to seal securely, leaving space for expansion of steam. Grill over *medium* coals till heated through, about 25 minutes. Before serving, remove bay leaf. Makes 4 servings.

WAX BEANS WITH MUSTARD SAUCE

1 tablespoon butter
1 tablespoon all-purpose flour
2 teaspoons prepared mustard
⅛ teaspoon pepper
1 cup milk
1 cup shredded American cheese
    (4 ounces)
1 teaspoon prepared horseradish
1 teaspoon lemon juice
2 16-ounce cans diagonal cut wax
    beans, drained

In heavy skillet melt butter over *medium-hot* coals; blend in flour, mustard, and pepper. Add milk all at once; cook and stir till thickened and bubbly, about 5 minutes.

Stir in shredded American cheese, horseradish, and lemon juice; stir till cheese melts. Stir in drained wax beans; heat through, about 4 minutes. Garnish with a parsley sprig, if desired. Makes 6 to 8 servings.

OUTDOOR VEGETABLE SKILLET

2 10-ounce packages frozen
    Brussels sprouts, thawed
2 medium tomatoes, peeled and
    chopped (1¼ cups)
1 cup frozen small whole onions,
    thawed
½ cup creamy French salad
    dressing
¼ teaspoon salt

Cut large Brussels sprouts in half. In shallow dish combine sprouts, tomatoes, and onions; pour salad dressing over all. Sprinkle with ¼ teaspoon salt. Cover; let stand at room temperature 2 hours, stirring mixture occasionally. Turn vegetable mixture into a heavy 10-

; place on grill. Simmer, covered, over *hot* coals
about 10 minutes. Uncover; simmer till vegetables are
tender, about 5 minutes more, stirring occasionally.
Serves 6.

HONEY-MUSTARD BEETS

1½ pounds fresh beets *or* 1
     16-ounce can sliced beets,
     drained
  2 tablespoons butter *or*
     margarine, melted
  1 tablespoon prepared mustard *or*
     Dijon-style mustard
  1 tablespoon honey
  1 teaspoon soy sauce
  ¼ cup snipped parsley

If using fresh beets, cut off all but 1 inch of stems and
roots; do not peel. Cook, covered, in boiling salted
water till tender, about 30 minutes. Drain; peel and
slice. Combine butter, mustard, honey, and soy. Tear
off a 36x18-inch piece of heavy-duty foil. Fold in half
to make an 18-inch square; fold up sides slightly. Place
beets in center of foil; pour honey sauce over all. Fold
edges of foil to seal securely, leaving space for expansion of steam. Grill over *medium-slow* coals till
heated through, about 20 minutes. Sprinkle with parsley. Serves 4.

Bread Fix-Ups and Quick Breads

PARSLEYED FRENCH SLICES

1 18-inch-long loaf French bread
¼ cup butter, softened
2 tablespoons snipped parsley
2 teaspoons prepared mustard
½ teaspoon barbecue spice

Cut bread in 1-inch diagonal slices, cutting to, but not through, bottom crust. Combine butter, parsley, mustard, and barbecue spice; spread between every other slice of bread. Wrap loosely in heavy-duty foil; place on edge of grill. Grill over *slow* coals till heated through, about 15 minutes, turning frequently. Makes 12 servings.

BARBECUED PUMPERNICKEL

1 1-pound round loaf
    pumpernickel
½ cup butter, softened
¼ cup grated Parmesan cheese
3 tablespoons mustard-mayonnaise
    sandwich and salad sauce
2 tablespoons snipped parsley

Cut bread in ½-inch-thick slices, cutting to, but not through, bottom crust. Combine butter, Parmesan, sandwich and salad sauce, and parsley; spread mixture between every other slice of bread. Make 1 lengthwise slice down center of loaf, cutting to, but not through, bottom crust. Wrap loaf loosely in heavy-duty foil. Grill over *slow* coals till heated through, 25 to 30 minutes. Serves 18.

GRILLED CHEESE ROLLS

1 3-ounce package cream cheese
½ cup shredded Cheddar cheese
2 tablespoons chopped green
    onion with tops
1 tablespoon milk
2 teaspoons Dijon-style mustard
12 dinner rolls

Soften cream cheese. Blend together cream cheese, Cheddar cheese, green onion, milk, and mustard. Split each dinner roll in half crosswise. Spread a little of the cheese mixture between each roll; reassemble rolls.

Wrap rolls loosely in heavy-duty foil. Grill over *slow* coals about 10 minutes, turning once. Makes 12 servings.

CARAWAY-CHEESE ROLLS

1 4-ounce container whipped
    cream cheese with pimiento
1 teaspoon caraway seed
1 teaspoon finely chopped green
    onion with tops
8 to 10 hard rolls

Mix cream cheese, caraway seed, and green onion. Split each roll lengthwise, cutting to, but not through, opposite side of roll. Spread rolls with cream cheese mixture. Wrap rolls loosely in heavy-duty foil. Grill over *medium* coals till hot, 8 to 10 minutes, turning once. Tear rolls in half; serve open face. Makes 8 to 10 servings.

CINNAMON-RAISIN FRENCH TOAST

2 beaten eggs
½ cup milk
1 tablespoon sugar
¼ teaspoon ground cinnamon
10 slices raisin bread
    Butter *or* margarine

In shallow bowl or pie plate combine eggs, milk, sugar, and cinnamon. Dip each slice bread on both sides into egg mixture. In heavy skillet melt *1 tablespoon* butter over *medium-hot* coals. Fry bread on both sides till golden brown, about 3 minutes per side. Add addi-

tional butter each time more bread is added. Serve
with butter. Pass maple-flavored syrup *or* applesauce,
if desired. Serves 5.

SWISS-BUTTERED RYE BREAD

¾ cup shredded process Swiss
   cheese
¼ cup butter, softened
2 tablespoons snipped parsley
½ teaspoon prepared mustard
⅛ teaspoon dried tarragon,
   crushed
10 slices rye bread

Cream together Swiss cheese, butter, parsley, mustard,
and tarragon. Spread cheese mixture on one side of
each bread slice. Place slices together, forming 5 sandwiches; stack sandwiches. Tear off a 24x18-inch piece
of heavy-duty foil; wrap stacked sandwiches loosely in
foil. Grill over *medium* coals till heated through, 20
to 25 minutes. Pull slices apart to serve. Makes 10
servings.

CHEESY BREAD KABOBS

1 5-ounce jar sharp American
   cheese spread
1 tablespoon butter, softened
1 tablespoon sliced green
   onion with tops
½ teaspoon dried tarragon,
   crushed
   Dash garlic powder
8 slices French bread

Combine the cheese spread, butter, green onion, tarragon, and garlic powder. Make two 4-layer sandwiches with the French bread slices, spreading cheese

mixture between slices and on top and bottom of stack. Cut each sandwich into quarters.

Using eight skewers, thread each sandwich quarter on a skewer. Grill over *medium* coals till lightly toasted, 6 to 7 minutes. Turn often. Makes 8 servings.

BARBECUED BREAD ITALIANO

2 cups packaged biscuit mix
⅔ cup milk
2 tablespoons grated Parmesan
    cheese
2 tablespoons snipped parsley
    Olive Topper
½ cup shredded Cheddar cheese
    (2 ounces)
2 tablespoons grated Parmesan
    cheese
    Paprika

Combine biscuit mix, milk, 2 tablespoons Parmesan, and parsley; stir just till dry ingredients are moistened. Spread dough evenly in a well-greased 12-inch heavy skillet. Spoon Olive Topper over dough; sprinkle shredded cheese and remaining Parmesan over all. Sprinkle edges with paprika. Place on hooded grill; lower hood. Grill over *medium* coals till done, 25 to 30 minutes. Serves 12.

Olive Topper: Combine ½ cup sliced pimiento-stuffed green olives, 2 tablespoons butter, melted; 2 tablespoons sliced green onion with tops, 1 teaspoon Worcestershire sauce, ½ teaspoon garlic powder, ½ teaspoon dried oregano; crushed, and 3 dashes hot pepper sauce.

MUFFIN MIX GRIDDLE CAKES

1 13½-ounce package blueberry
    muffin mix
2 beaten eggs
⅓-⅔ cup water
2 tablespoons cooking oil
⅔ cup honey
⅓ cup maple-flavored syrup
    Butter *or* margarine

Combine muffin mix, beaten eggs, and ⅓ to ⅔ cup water
(use ⅓ cup water for thick pancakes, ⅔ cup for thin).
Beat till smooth; stir in oil. (If using blueberry mix,
fold in blueberries.) Preheat lightly greased heavy
skillet or griddle over *hot* coals for 2 to 3 minutes. For
each cake, spread 1 tablespoon batter on prepared
skillet or griddle. Cook over *hot* coals till browned,
about 1½ minutes per side. Meanwhile, heat together
honey and syrup; serve syrup and butter with pancakes. Makes 36.

Appetizers and Desserts

BARBECUE-STYLE RACLETTE

1½ cups shredded Swiss cheese
1 cup shredded Gruyère cheese
1 4½-ounce can deviled ham
2 tablespoons chopped pimiento
2 tablespoons snipped parsley
2 teaspoons caraway seed
1 teaspoon prepared mustard
1 teaspoon Worcestershire sauce
⅛ teaspoon pepper
¼ cup milk
¼ cup butter, softened
1 medium head cauliflower,
    broken into flowerets and
    sliced (4 cups)
4 dill pickles, cut in wedges
1 cup cherry tomatoes
1 loaf French bread, sliced

In small mixing bowl combine Swiss cheese, Gruyère, deviled ham, pimiento, parsley, caraway, mustard, Worcestershire, and pepper. Heat milk just to boiling; immediately pour over cheese mixture. Beat at low speed of electric mixer 2 minutes, scraping sides of bowl constantly.

Beat mixture at high speed till nearly smooth, about 5 minutes, scraping bowl occasionally. Beat in softened butter. Cover and chill at least 1 hour. Shape cheese mixture into sixteen 1-inch cubes; place on waxed paper on baking sheet. Cover; chill several hours or overnight. Keep chilled till ready to serve. To serve, place each cheese cube on a fondue fork or pair of skewers. Hold over *very hot* coals just till cheese softens; spread over vegetables and bread. Serves 8.

CRAB-BACON BITES

1 7½-ounce can crab meat
1 beaten egg
¼ cup tomato juice
½ cup fine dry bread crumbs
1 tablespoon grated Parmesan
cheese
1 tablespoon finely chopped
green onion with tops
1 tablespoon lemon juice
¼ teaspoon salt
¼ teaspoon Worcestershire sauce
Dash bottled hot pepper sauce
12 slices bacon
Nonsitick vegetable
spray coating

Drain, flake, and remove cartilage from crab meat; set aside. In bowl combine egg, tomato juice, bread crumbs, Parmesan cheese, green onion, lemon juice, salt, Worcestershire, and hot pepper sauce. Add crab meat; mix well. Cut bacon slices in half. In skillet partially cook bacon; drain on paper toweling. Shape crab mixture into 24 logs, about 1½ inches long. Wrap each log with a half slice bacon; fasten securely with wooden picks. Spray cold grill with nonstick vegetable spray coating. Grill the logs over *hot* coals till evenly browned, about 10 minutes, turning several times. Makes 24 appetizers.

GRILLED STUFFED MUSHROOMS

24 fresh medium mushrooms
¼ cup chopped green onion with
    tops
3 tablespoons butter
2 teaspoons all-purpose flour
½ teaspoon dried marjoram,
    crushed
¼ cup dry white wine
½ cup finely chopped fully
    cooked ham
1 tablespoon snipped parsley

Remove stems from mushrooms; reserve caps. Chop stems. In saucepan cook chopped stems and green onion in *1 tablespoon* of the butter just till tender. Blend in flour, marjoram, and dash pepper; add wine. Cook and stir till thickened and bubbly; stir in ham and parsley. Stuff mushroom caps with ham mixture. Place stuffed mushrooms on a 20x18-inch piece of heavy-duty foil; dot with remaining 2 tablespoons butter. Fold edges of foil to seal securely; place packet on grill. Grill over *medium* coals till mushrooms are tender, 15 to 20 minutes. Makes 24.

DEVILED CHICKEN LIVER KABOBS

Boiling water
16 fresh large mushrooms
 2 tablespoons Dijon-style
    mustard
 1 tablespoon catsup
 1 tablespoon butter *or* margarine
 2 teaspoons Worcestershire
    sauce
 ¼ teaspoon onion powder
    Dash cayenne
 ½ pound chicken livers, halved
    (about 16 halves)
16 cherry tomatoes
    Cooking oil

Pour some boiling water over mushrooms in bowl. Let
stand 1 minute; drain well. In saucepan stir together
Dijon-style mustard, catsup, butter, Worcestershire,
onion powder, and cayenne; mix well. Heat and stir
over *medium-hot* coals just till butter melts. Move pan
to edge of grill to keep the mixture warm.

Meanwhile, thread mushrooms, chicken livers, and
cherry tomatoes *each* on separate skewers. Grill mushrooms and chicken livers over *medium-hot* coals about
3 minutes. Add the tomato skewers; grill about 3 minutes longer. Turn and brush frequently with mustard
mixture; brush vegetables with a little oil. (Be care-
ful not to overcook.) Remove livers and vegetables
from skewers; serve on wooden picks. Makes 16 appetizers.

MARINATED SHRIMP APPETIZERS

    2 pounds fresh *or* frozen large
         shrimp, shelled and deveined
    ½ cup cooking oil
    ½ cup lime juice
    3 tablespoons dry white wine
    1 tablespoon snipped chives
    1 clove garlic, minced
    1½ teaspoons salt
    ½ teaspoon dried dillweed
      Several dashes bottled hot
         pepper sauce

Thaw shrimp, if frozen. Place in shallow baking dish.
Combine cooking oil, lime juice, wine, chives, garlic,
salt, dillweed, and hot pepper sauce. Pour marinade
mixture over shrimp. Cover; refrigerate 4 to 6 hours
or overnight. Occasionally spoon marinade over
shrimp.

Remove the shrimp, reserving marinade. Thread
shrimp on skewers or place in a wire grill basket. Grill
over *hot* coals till done, 8 to 10 minutes, turning and
brushing often with reserved marinade. Serve on
wooden picks. Makes about 30 appetizers.

TERIYAKI APPETIZER RIBS

    4 pounds meaty pork spareribs,
         sawed in half across bones
    ½ cup soy sauce
    2 tablespoons cooking oil
    2 tablespoons lemon juice
    1 tablespoon brown sugar
    2 cloves garlic, minced
    1 teaspoon ground ginger
    ¼ teaspoon pepper
    2 tablespoons honey

Cut meat in 2-rib portions. Mix soy, oil, lemon juice, brown sugar, garlic, ginger, and pepper. Place ribs in shallow baking dish; pour marinade mixture over. Cover; refrigerate 4 to 6 hours or overnight. Occasionally spoon marinade over. Remove ribs, reserving marinade. Grill over *slow* coals, bone side down, about 25 minutes. (Add less meaty ribs after 10 minutes of grilling.) Turn ribs, meaty side down, and grill 15 to 20 minutes more. Meanwhile, stir honey into reserved marinade; brush frequently over ribs during last 5 minutes. Makes about 26.

OVER-THE-COALS POPCORN

¼ cup butter *or* margarine,
    melted
¾ teaspoon chili powder
¼ teaspoon garlic salt
    Dash cayenne
½ cup unpopped popcorn

In saucepan combine butter, chili powder, garlic salt, and cayenne. Set on edge of grill to keep warm. Tear off two 36x18-inch pieces of heavy-duty foil. Fold each in half to make an 18-inch square. Fold up sides, using fist to form pouches. In center of each, place ¼ *cup* of the popcorn. Bring corners of foil together; squeeze tightly to seal edges, leaving room for popcorn to pop. Tie string securely around top of pouches; tie each pouch to a long-handled barbecue tool or green stick. Hold pouches over, but not touching *hot* coals; shake till corn is popped, 6 to 8 minutes. Open pouches; pour butter mixture over popped corn, tossing to coat. Makes 9 cups.

SHERRIED PEACHES

½ cup cream sherry *or* port
¼ cup sugar
2 tablespoons apricot preserves
1 tablespoon lemon juice
⅛ teaspoon ground cinnamon
   Dash ground cloves
   Dash salt
6 peaches, peeled, halved,
     and pitted (1½ pounds)

Stir together cream sherry or port, sugar, preserves, lemon juice, cinnamon, cloves, and salt; set aside.

Tear off six 10x18-inch pieces of heavy-duty foil. Fold up sides of each piece of foil, using fist to form pouches. Place *two* peach halves in each foil pouch. Pour about 2 *tablespoons* of the sherry mixture over the peaches in each pouch; fold edges of foil to seal securely. Grill over *medium* coals till heated through, 15 to 20 minutes. Makes 6 servings.

CHERRY-PEAR SKILLET COBBLER

1 package refrigerated caramel
     Danish rolls with nuts
     (8 rolls)
½ teaspoon finely shredded
     orange peel
¼ cup orange juice
¼ teaspoon ground cinnamon
1 21-ounce can cherry *or*
     strawberry pie filling
3 medium pears, peeled, cored,
     and sliced (2½ cups)
   Light cream *or* vanilla ice
   cream

In 10-inch heavy skillet with tight-fitting lid, crumble sugar-nut mixture from refrigerated caramel rolls; add orange peel, orange juice, and cinnamon. Stir in cherry or strawberry pie filling and pears; cover. Grill over *medium-slow* coals till mixture is bubbly and pears are nearly tender, about 10 minutes.

Separate caramel rolls; arrange rolls, cut side down, atop hot mixture in skillet. Cover; cook till rolls are done, about 20 minutes longer. Serve warm with cream or ice cream. Makes 8 servings.

RAISIN-STUFFED APPLES

4 large baking apples
½ cup raisins
½ cup dry sherry *or* water
2 tablespoons chopped walnuts
2 tablespoons brown sugar
2 tablespoons chopped
   maraschino cherries
⅛ teaspoon ground cinnamon
⅛ teaspoon ground cloves
⅛ teaspoon ground nutmeg
1 tablespoon butter *or* margarine
   Vanilla ice cream

Core apples; enlarge each opening slightly. Place each apple on a 12x18-inch piece of heavy-duty foil. Combine raisins, sherry or water, walnuts, sugar, cherries, and spices. Divide filling among apples. Dot with butter or margarine. Bring foil up around apples; seal loosely. Grill over *slow* coals for about 1 hour. Open foil; serve with a scoop of vanilla ice cream. Serves 4.

GRILLED FRESH FRUIT

½ cup sugar
¼ cup butter *or* margarine
2 tablespoons brandy *or*
  lemon juice
½ teaspoon ground cinnamon
  Any fresh fruit as listed in chart
  below

In saucepan combine sugar, butter, brandy or lemon juice, and cinnamon. Place on grill; heat and stir over *medium* coals till glaze mixture boils. Remove from grill. Shape a piece of heavy-duty foil into the shape of a shallow pan; place on grill. Place fruit in foil pan. Grill fruit over *medium* coals till heated through, turning and brushing often with glaze mixtture. See chart below for grilling time. Serve fruit warm; pass remaining glaze.

Fruit	Grilling Time
Apples, cored and quartered	30 minutes
Bananas, peeled and halved crosswise	6 minutes
Nectarines, halved and pitted	12 minutes
Oranges, peeled and sliced	10 minutes
Peaches (freestone), peeled, halved, and pitted	16 minutes
Pears, cored and halved or quartered	18 minutes
Pineapple chunks or spears	6 minutes

BARBECUE BASICS

Today, more people than ever before are finding that barbecuing is great fun. And with this increase in popularity comes a wide variety of new equipment to make outdoor cooking carefree. But unless you understand the basics, cookouts are not fun or easy. This chapter explains small equipment, grills, and charcoal cooking. Whether you're a first-timer or an experienced outdoor chef, you're sure to pick up some helpful pointers.

Equipment for Cookouts

SMALL EQUIPMENT

After purchasing the grill, limit your selection of other tools to small essentials that simplify barbecuing. Listed below are items that every serious barbecuer should purchase, and also some optional gear. Not illustrated but equally necessary to have on hand are long skewers, salt and pepper shakers, a carving knife, and heavy-duty foil.

(1) Long-handled tongs—no chef does without two pairs, one for food, and one for the coals; (2) a basting brush to swish on sauces; (3) a fork to help keep a grip on the food; and (4) a multi-purpose turner. (All with long handles to keep you a safe distance from the coals.)

Other good investments for outdoor chefs include (5) a wire grill basket that adjusts to the thickness of the food; (6) spit basket that attaches to a spit rod; (7) rib rack; (8) potholders and asbestos mitts; and (9) a meat thermometer to help ensure that the internal temperature or meat and poultry is done to your liking. (A thermometer is especially useful in outdoor cooking where meat may look done on the outside and be undercooked on the inside.

Also, keep (10) a plant sprinkler or a pump-spray bottle filled with water to put out flare-ups, and don't forget to have (11) a supply of extra coals ready to use.

BARBECUE GRILLS

It's unbelievable the amount of outdoor cooking equipment that's available for today's barbecue enthusiast. Grills come in many sizes, styles, and prices with features to suit the needs of experienced backyard chefs and novices alike. The more expensive models offer the added conveniences of motor-driven rotisseries and skewers, storage drawers, utensil racks, and cutting boards. The following pointers will help you decide which type and model of grill are right for you.

BEST BUYS FOR THE BEGINNER

Start your barbecuing career with a small brazier or a lightweight folding unit. Either style is easy to use, convenient to store, and inexpensive. Experiment with using foil drip pans, placement of coals, and different types of food cooked over a variety of coal temperatures. After a season or two of barbecuing, you'll know whether you are an avid barbecue fan or only an "occasional backyard chef."

SELECTING THE RIGHT GRILL

After you learn the basic techniques of barbecuing on a small brazier grill, you may want to consider buying a more elaborate model. Which type of grill you purchase depends on the amount of money you want to invest and how much barbecuing you want to do. If you barbecue infrequently or only with small groups, there's no need to invest in an expensive model. You may decide the grill you started with does everything desired. But even if you need a more elaborate unit, don't cast aside the old one. The first grill makes a handy unit for grilling appetizers, breads, or hot desserts. Even use the unit to store hot coals for supplementing long cooking on the main grill.

TYPES OF BARBECUE GRILLS

Brazier grills—Lightweight, inexpensive, and easy to use, the brazier is the most popular grill on the market. Options available include models ranging from simple fold-up units to elaborate three-legged ones on wheels with half hoods, rotisseries, and air dampers. Large braziers have a lever or crank that regulates the distance between the grate and coals. This aids in controlling the heat.

Hibachis—Apartment dwellers or anyone cramped for space who need a small outdoor grill will find the sturdy hibachis just the thing. These small, efficient grills come complete with adjustable grates, air dampers, and coal racks to let ashes sift to the bottom. Even backyard chefs with elaborate equipment find this well-designed grill great for the appetizer table or an intimate dinner for two.

Kettle and wagon grills—Although relatively expensive compared to the lighter-weight braziers, the kettle and wagon grills are far more versatile and usually constructed with heavier materials. The kettle, semispherical in shape, features a coal rack near the bottom and grate in the middle. The lid then is the top half of the sphere. Wagons, on the other hand, are rectangular in shape, with options such as full hoods, smoke chambers, warming ovens or racks, cutting boards, and built-in fire starters.

The shape of kettles and wagons differs from brand to brand, but they all feature important air dampers both in the bottom and in the lid to control ventilation. Open these dampers when you need a hot fire or close them partway to cool down the coals.

Similar cooking techniques are available in kettle and wagon grills. Lid up, the kettles and wagons become braziers, even offering motor-driven rotisseries and skewers. Lid down, these grills are effective ovens, with heat controlled by air dampers. If you desire a smoky taste, set the grill up as for an oven and add dampened hickory chips to the hot coals.

Smokers—As their name implies, smokers give foods an appetizing smoky flavor after many hours of cooking. Like all barbecue equipment, the various smokers range from the relatively simple to elaborate units. A popular style is the small portable domed smoke oven. The meat cooks directly over a bed of smoldering coals, similar to smoking in covered kettle or wagon grills.

Another portable model is completely open at the

bottom, providing good air circulation. A tray of coals supported by pegs heats the meat and dampened hickory chips plus a small pan of water between it and the grate. The heated water adds moisture to the smoke and keeps the meat moist during the long hours of cooking.

There's another, more elaborate unit, the Chinese smoker. Whether the unit is a permanent brick structure or a movable metal one, the smoker is L-shaped with an upright chimney. The meat hangs on racks or hooks in the chimney away from the bed of coals and the food cooks slowly in the hot smoke.

Remember, smokers only cook the food—they are not food curing and preserving equipment. Refrigerate any food leftover from smoker cooking.

Gas and electric grills—The newest in barbecue grills feature gas or electricity as the heat source instead of charcoal. Gas and most electric models work on the principle of radiant heat. Volcanic pumice or ceramic briquets, placed on racks between the heat source and grate, heat to a desired temperature. It's the heat radiating from them that actually cooks the food producing an appetizing flavor and appearance.

Gas and electric models are convenient versions of the kettle and wagon grills. Quick and easy to start plus better heat control are factors contributing greatly to their increasing popularity. Permanently installed gas grills use natural or LP gas. Portable gas grills use only LP gas, which comes in tanks of various sizes.

Gas and electric grills differ greatly from brand to brand, it's important to understand how your particular model works. Read all the manufacturer's instructions.

Charcoal Cooking Know-How

You undoubtedly know an outdoor chef who barbecues delightful meals atop the grill. The food smells tantalizing and tastes even better. And everything always remains under control—never a flare-up, never a burnt pork chop. This expertise doesn't happen by accident. Chances are, the backyard barbecue expert you know has taken the time to master the techniques involved in barbecuing.

Following are some pointers that will help you get the most out of your equipment and the food you barbecue.

PREPARING THE FIREBOX

Before you go out and fire up the grill, no matter what type of equipment it is, always read the manufacturer's instructions. The firebox may need a foundation for the charcoal fire. (A) protect the brazier grill's firebox with a lining of heavy-duty foil, then top with 1 inch of pea gravel, coarse grit, or expanded mica insulation pellets. This bedding foundation allows some air in under the briquets so the coals will burn better. It also protects the firebox from the intense heat of the coals, distributes the heat more evenly, and reduces flare-ups by absorbing dripping fats and the meat juices.

After you've used the grill a dozen times, the liner will be full of greasy drippings. Gravel or grit bedding can be washed, dried thoroughly, and used again. If you have used insulation pellets, discard and replace with new.

KEEP THE BRIQUETS TO A MINIMUM

Beginning chefs often overdo it and build too big a bed of coals. Estimate how many briquets you'll need for the size of the grill and the type and amount of food to be grilled. It's unnecessary to cover the entire grill area for a few frankfurters. Large thick cuts of meat require more charcoal than do thin steaks and burgers.

If you plan to barbecue for more than one hour,

extra briquets need to be added to the bed of coals to maintain its proper cooking temperature. Place a dozen cold briquets around the outer edge of the hot bed of coals. Then, as needed, rake them into the other coals. Or, have a metal bucket or small portable brazier of glowing coals ready at the side of your barbecue unit.

GETTING THE CHARCOAL STARTED

Pile the number of briquets needed into a pyramid or mound in the center of the firebox. Drizzle liquid lighter or jelly fire starter over the whole surface of the charcoal. Wait 1 minute, then ignite with a match. (Never use gasoline or kerosene to start charcoal. Gasoline is much too dangerous, and kerosene adds an unpleasant taste to your food.) For faster starting, use an electrical fire starter. Place the briquets over the coil, plug in the starter, and in 5 to 15 minutes the coals will be ready. Remove the coil to a heatproof location, and distribute coals around the firebox to suit the kind of food you'll be cooking.

Don't start barbecuing too soon; the coals need to burn about 20 to 30 minutes. The charcoal is ready for grilling when it dies down to a glow and no areas of black show. Live coals look ash-gray by day and glow red after dark. A thin layer of gray ash smothers the coals. You'll need to tap the coals frequently to loosen ashes so the coals can breathe and burn properly.

ARRANGING THE HOT COALS

When the coals are ready, use a fire rake or long-handled tongs to spread the coals in a single layer. The arrangement of the hot coals depends on the kind of grill used and the type of food being barbecued.

(B) For spit-roasting spareribs, roasts, leg of lamb, or poultry, use a ring of coals to grill. Position the foil drip pan directly under the meat, and then spread the coals in a circle all around the firebox.

(C) In a covered grill for barbecuing large pieces of meat, make a foil drip pan a little larger than the meat. Place drip pan in center of firebox and pile coals on both sides of pan. Replace the grate and set meat directly over the drip pan. Lower the hood.

(D) Barbecue steaks, chops, and other foods that are grilled flat by raking coals over the entire firebox. Place the coals about ½ inch apart for even heat.

Grill kabobs by lining up hot coals in parallel rows in the firebox plus coals around edge of grill. Stagger skewers on the grate directly above spaces between briquet rows so meat fats will not drip on coals.

DETERMINE COOKING TEMPERATURE OF THE COALS

(E) Hold your hand palm-side down just above hot coals at the height the food will be cooking. Begin counting "one thousand one, one thousand two;" if you need to withdraw your hand after two seconds the coals are hot, three seconds for medium-hot coals, four seconds for medium coals, and five or six seconds for slow coals.

ADJUSTING THE HEAT FOR THE RIGHT TEMPERATURE

When the coals are too hot, either raise the grill's gate, lower the firebox, close the air vents, or simply remove some of the hot briquets. Increase the temperature of the coals in the grill's firebox by tapping the ashes off the burning coals with tongs, moving the coals closer together, lowering the grate, raising the firebox, or opening the vents to allow more air to circulate through the grill.

CONTROLLING THE FLARE-UPS

Reduce flare-ups when meat fat drips on the coals by spacing farther apart or removing a few to cut down on the heat. Keep a pump-spray bottle filled with water handy. Sprinkle a little water on the flare-ups— don't soak the coals.

SAVE AND REUSE THE CHARCOAL

After barbecuing don't let briquets just burn away. If using a covered grill, lower hood and close air vents. Or, if you own an open-type unit, use tongs to transfer hot coals to a metal pail half full of water. Drain and spread the charcoal onto a stack of papers to dry. The charcoal must be absolutely dry or it will not relight.

CLEANING UP THE BARBECUE GRILL

It's easier to clean the grates right after barbecuing. Read all the cleaning, care, and storage directions supplied with your equipment before using any cleaning products or abrasives. Fill sink with hot, sudsy water and put the grill's grate in to soak. Later, a few swipes with a wet cloth will clean the grate.

If the grate is too large to fit in a sink, cover with wet paper towels or wet newspapers while you eat. Place the hot grate on one stack of well-soaked papers, then cover with second. Burned-on food usually washes right off with a wet cloth. Use scouring or abrasive-type pads and/or a stiff grill brush for the stubborn spots.

INDEX

Barbecue Tips